GRILL
MASTER

Fred Thompson

Photography
Ray Kachatorian

weldon**owen**

Contents

Get Your Grill On

And then there was fire. People have been cooking their meals over flame for eons, but over time the process has changed from a necessity to a special treat. Many of us have memories of backyard burgers and hot dogs, of steaks sizzling on a hot grate, or of the mountain of smoky ribs that fueled gatherings of family and friends. Grilling adds pleasure to our lives in an uncomplicated, relaxing way.

I can't remember a time when a grill wasn't important in my life. I have early memories of my uncle roasting a whole hog for Labor Day family reunions, and of my dad, every Saturday night, rain or shine, tending rib-eye steaks over the coals while he nursed a bourbon and ginger ale. When he finally let me turn the steaks, I was hooked. Growing up in the South, where grilling is king, has allowed me not only to experiment with various techniques and ingredients, but also to collaborate and commiserate with others who are just as intent as I am on perfecting the backyard craft. I've talked with old-time pit masters and barbecue champions and watched and listened for tips that would improve my efforts, and I have been rewarded. Sometimes I think I'm obsessed with coaxing the very best flavors out of my grill, but heck, even the road to the best is pretty doggone tasty.

The goal of this book is to help you achieve greater success with your grill, whether it's charcoal or gas, round or square, little or big. You'll find recipes for the basic proteins—beef, lamb, pork, poultry, and seafood—as well as some surprising grilled items like pizza and quesadillas. There are detailed tips and recipes to ensure perfect results for the classics, like steaks, cheeseburgers, pork chops, smoked ribs, barbecued chicken, and fish fillets. And so your grilled main course is never alone on the plate, I have also included an abundance of side dishes to complete the feast in style.

If I'm in your neighborhood and you're grilling up my recipe for an Italian porterhouse steak, please invite me over; it's one of my favorites. I'm crazy for oysters cooked on the grill, too, and I am proud to say my baby back rib recipe is just awesome. Also, try the grilled pizzas and the many great grilled veggie combinations—you'll be happy you did. Gosh, there are so many great recipes, it's hard to choose favorites. And just thinking about the tastes that lie ahead is making me hungry, so let's start grilling!

Fred Thompson

GRILLING BASICS

This section is your go-to resource for all things grilling, from tools and methods to my top tips for success. Let's kick this off with a few words about the most important tool you can have in your grilling arsenal: the grill. Whether you opt for charcoal or gas, a big, round kettle or a small, square hibachi—or you wind up with more than one model—you'll find that few cooking tools are as versatile or can flavor food as successfully as an outdoor grill.

The Charcoal Grill Charcoal grills come in many shapes and sizes, from the small disposable picnic grill to the party-sized ranch kettle model. In any case, look for a well-built, high-grade steel grill with a lid and with at least two vents to control airflow and temperature. The most useful size and model is the fairly standard 22-inch (55-cm) kettle. It efficiently and quickly grills cuts of meat and seafood over a hot or medium-hot fire and can also be converted to accommodate longer-cooking foods that require low temperatures. If you plan to do a lot of smoking, look for a grill with a side fire box.

The Gas Grill Gas grills run the gamut from a no-frills cart to a gadget-filled mini-kitchen. Here's the skinny: two burners are a must, but if you plan to do indirect cooking, three burners will make life easier and give you better control. Don't get ramped up on BTUs: 35,000 should be plenty. Instead, look at how the heat is diffused: angled metal plates covering the burners are particularly effective and reduce flare-ups. Shoot for cooking racks that are either stainless steel or stainless steel with a powder-paint finish. If your grill has an infrared burner, know that it will cook hotter than regular gas.

The Smoker Smoker grills—which can be round, vertical, or bullet shaped and fired by gas or charcoal—are designed to give you the best result when what you want is low, slow cooking. Most smokers include a water pan to keep the temperature low and the food moist, and often call for wood chunks, which burn more slowly than wood chips. Each model works a little differently, so read your owner's manual for directions.

Other Grill Types You'll find a wide array of portable grills on the market that fold up nicely for travel, yet deliver the performance of a regular grill. If you are a tailgater, check these out. Compact bucket grills have been around since the 1950s and with good reason: they may be the best portable charcoal grills available. Ceramic egg-shaped grills have a cultlike following and deliver great results, especially when used for smoking.

Come on Baby, Light My Fire Pit

Just the smell of smoking wood is enough to bring folks together, but it's also a fun and exciting way to cook food, if you have the right set-up. Not really designed for long-cooking items, a fire pit can quickly put a hickory, oak, or apple flavor nicely into a steak. Here's how to set one up.

1 Find a spot that's flat, dry, and clear of buildings, tree branches, and brush. The surface of the pit should be nonflammable (a metal fire ring is ideal).

2 Line the bottom and sides of the pit with large stones to retain the heat and keep the fire contained.

3 Use hardwood, like oak, hickory, or fruitwood; stay away from softwood like pine or fir. For more even burning, you can mix the wood with charcoal briquettes.

4 It's easiest to light the wood and/or charcoal in a chimney starter (page 14) and then transfer it to the pit, but you can also arrange the wood in the pit and use some kindling to get the fire going. Place a grill grate securely at least 4 inches (10 cm) above the coals. Let the wood burn down until the embers are covered in ash before you start grilling. Have water or a fire extinguisher on hand in case you need to put out flames (be careful of steam burns if using water).

Grilling Gear

It's hard to keep track of all the grilling gadgets available nowadays. Some you need, like a chimney starter if you have a charcoal grill. Others can be useful and/or fun, like rib racks, clip-on lights, and gas-tank gauges. Here's the lowdown on what I think is essential.

Basic Tools A long-handled brush with rustproof bristles is indispensable for cleaning the grill grate: brass bristles are good for porcelain-enamel grates, steel for cast-iron grates. Use it to brush the hot grate both before and after cooking. Employ a smaller, more angled brush for cleaning between the grate bars. You also need a few pairs of sturdy metal tongs of various lengths and a medium-length spatula for turning foods.

Thermometers The best and easiest way to test large meat and poultry cuts for doneness is with an instant-read thermometer. Simply insert the probe into the thickest part of the protein, away from any bone, and in seconds, it registers the temperature. It's also important to keep track of the temperature inside the grill, especially when you'll be cooking food for a long period of time. Specialized grill thermometers attached to the grate can be wildly inaccurate. A good oven thermometer is a better choice. A laser thermometer is even more reliable, but also costly.

Protective Gear Burnt fingers don't look good on anyone—especially a grill master. Keep an oven mitt or pot holder made of heavy quilted cotton close by to protect your hands from the grill's intense heat. Leather gloves made for grilling or wrangling fireplace fires are also nice to have.

Basting Brush Cotton mop–style basting brushes look good during barbecue contests, but they are hard to clean and not very sanitary. Pastry brushes are usually so short that your

fingers get toasty when you apply sauce, plus they are tough to clean. Brushes with long stainless-steel handles and silicone bristles work beautifully, both at the grill and the sink.

Skewers Wood or metal, round or flat—folks are divided on which skewers are best. My advice is to buy a set of flat metal skewers at least 8 inches (20 cm) long. The metal conducts heat nicely, which helps your food cook more quickly and evenly. If you opt for wood, soak the skewers in water—or in beer, wine, or fruit juice for extra flavor—for at least 30 minutes before using.

Baskets, Plates, and Screens Hinged grill baskets, plates, and screens come in handy for delicate foods that are difficult to turn, such as fish fillets, or for foods that might fall through the grill grate, such as asparagus. A plate is a perforated metal sheet, and a screen is a fine wire mesh in a metal frame. Brush all three with oil to prevent sticking and preheat over direct heat before adding the food.

Chimney Starter A chimney starter is the most efficient way to light your charcoal or hardwood fire for a charcoal grill. For a medium-sized grill, look for a starter that is at least 7½ inches (19 cm) in diameter and 12 inches (30 cm) tall.

Drip Pan A drip pan is set on the grill bed of a charcoal grill under large cuts of meat and poultry to capture dripping fat and juices, preventing flare-ups. It is also indispensable if gravy is on the menu. Any disposable aluminum pan as long and as wide as the item being grilled and 2 inches (5 cm) deep will work.

Smoker Box A smoker box is a heavy, vented metal container for holding soaked wood chips or herbs in a gas grill. If your grill doesn't have one, you can fashion your own box out of aluminum foil (see page 19).

Grilling Methods

Dozens of different grill models, both charcoal and gas, are on the market. But when it comes to putting them to work, the same basic grilling methods apply: direct heat, indirect heat, and smoking.

Direct-Heat Grilling For this method, the food is placed directly over the fire of a charcoal grill or the heat elements of a gas grill. The food cooks relatively quickly—usually in less than 25 minutes—over intense heat, which sears and caramelizes the surface, boosting the flavor. Some grill cooks use a lid to reduce flare-ups and control the temperature. Others insist the grill be left uncovered at all times. (For my position on lid use, see page 13). If you plan to swab the food with a sugary sauce, do it just before it comes off the grill so the sauce doesn't burn from exposure to the intense heat.

GOOD CUTS TO USE Burgers, steaks, chops, pork tenderloins, boneless chicken pieces, kebabs, fish fillets, shrimp, vegetables

Indirect-Heat Grilling Here, the food is placed away from the heat source, so it cooks from reflected heat. In a charcoal grill that means arranging the hot coals so that either the center of the grill bed or one side of the bed is not delivering direct heat, and then placing the food above that space and covering the grill. In a gas grill, that means turning off one or more burners, placing the food over the turned-off burner(s), and keeping the lid on. Use this method for foods that cook for more than 25 minutes. Sometimes you are grilling foods that benefit from a good sear and also take longer than 25 minutes to cook. Barbecued bone-in chicken is a good example. I like to sear the pieces over direct heat until they are nicely browned, and then move them to the cooler area of the grill, cover the grill, and let them finish cooking in the reflected heat.

GOOD CUTS TO USE Beef roasts, leg of lamb, thick-cut pork chops, pork loins, whole chickens, bone-in chicken pieces

Smoking Indirect-heat grilling is also used for smoking and barbecuing. The grill setup is basically the same, with a few additional components: smoke and steam. Soaked wood chips or chunks provide the smoke, and a drip pan filled with water provides the steam. And you're cooking the food at a very low temperature for a long period of time (usually over an hour) to break down the proteins in the meat.

GOOD CUTS TO USE Brisket, ribs, pulled pork, turkey

For specific instructions for these three grilling methods on both charcoal and gas grills, turn to pages 16–19.

True Barbecue

Hard-core barbecue enthusiasts may sneer at your kettle or gas grill and proclaim that you can't make real barbecue without a smoker. This might be true, but I think you can come awfully close. Barbecue is all about smoke and very low heat. Once you get the hang of adding wood chips or chunks to your grill and keeping the temperature steady, you will be a believer, too. It starts with soaking wood chips, and then setting up your grill, charcoal or gas, for indirect heat. Check the temperature inside the grill. It should be 200° to 225°F (95° to 110°C) and never hotter than 325°F (165°C). Use the vents on a charcoal grill or the controls on a gas grill to regulate the heat. Add a small pan of liquid to the grill grate and keep it filled. It creates steam so the meat doesn't dry out. Keep the grill covered so you don't lose precious heat. Then sit back and relax as a tough cut of meat transforms into a tender mouthful.

Put a Lid on It

Grilling experts debate this question all the time. I have found that for most home grillers using the lid is the way to go for nearly every type of food. Covering the grill creates a convection-like heat that cooks foods evenly and more quickly. Of course, it is absolutely critical to cover the grill when grilling with indirect heat and when smoking meat. And even though you don't have to cover the grill for direct heat grilling, I figure why not pass along some of that great gentle heat that the lid provides, along with a shorter cooking time? You can still sear your steaks with the grill uncovered, and then cover it so they cook perfectly.

Grilling with Charcoal

Grilling with live fire, aka charcoal, still holds the heart of the grill master. Do the results taste better? Possibly. But charcoal loyalty may be more about the satisfaction you feel for your effort than about taste. And, of course, with just a bag of charcoal, you can grill just about anywhere.

Choosing the Fuel Standard charcoal briquettes deliver the most even heat and steady burn rate, but they are pumped full of ingredients that are not natural. All-natural hardwood briquettes burn a bit hotter and also burn cleaner. Natural lump hardwood, the real thing, burns superhot (great for steaks), and burns even cleaner. Given the choice, I think hardwood briquettes are the way to go, because they are easy to work with and produce quality results. If you are grilling food for four people, use about 20 briquettes, which will burn for about 1 hour. If you are grilling double that amount of food, double the number of briquettes. For indirect and low and slow cooking, calculate the cooking time, then start with 80 briquettes, which should last for about 2 hours. Add about 40 briquettes directly to the fire after about 1½ hours, or start more briquettes in your chimney starter and add to the fire after about 2 hours.

Lighting the Coals Lightly stuff newspaper (two or three sheets) in the bottom (under the grate) of a chimney starter. Don't use too much or you will smother the fire. Pour the briquettes or hardwood chunks over the grate, filling the chimney, then light the paper. The fire will burn upward and ignite the fuel. In 15 to 20 minutes, the coals should be covered with gray ash and glowing. Pour the hot coals onto the fire bed of the grill.

Controlling the Heat Before you can control the heat, you need to know how to measure it. The low-tech way is to hold your hand about 6 inches (15 cm) above the fire and count: one Mississippi, two Mississippi, three Mississippi, and so on. A count of one is a hot fire, two is a medium-hot fire, and three is a medium fire. A count of five is just right for smoky barbecue. On a thermometer, 450°F (230°C) is hot, 400°F (200°C) is medium-hot, and 350°F (180°C) is medium. A temperature of around 225°F (110°C) means the grill is ready for barbecuing and smoking. To control the heat, move the food closer or farther away from the fire, or adjust the vents, wider for more heat or narrower for less.

Flavoring Your Fire

You can use smoldering wood chips or chunks to flavor food as it cooks on a grill. Here are some flavor-and-food combinations to get you started: Intensely flavored hickory, oak, mesquite, and pecan chips or chunks complement chicken, turkey, pork, or beef. Hickory is too intense to use alone; temper it with a milder wood. Moderately intense fruitwoods like apple, cherry, and plum are a bit sweet. Pair them with pork, salmon, game birds, chicken, or anything with a sweet sauce. Mild alder wood is perfect for fish. You can use herbs, too—rosemary and lamb, basil and chicken, pork and bay—or grapevine cuttings. Always soak the woods and herbs in water before using. See page 17 to learn how to add wood chips to a charcoal grill.

Dealing with Flare-ups

Foods with a high-fat content—steaks, burgers, chops—usually cause flare-ups. You want the food to develop a little char, but it shouldn't look (or taste) like a burnt marshmallow.

One solution to this problem is to punch holes in a sheet of aluminum foil and slip it between the food and the grill grate. Or, you can douse the flare-ups with water from a spray bottle (but watch for steam burns).

Two better options: move the food to a cooler part of the grill, or close the vents a bit to reduce the fire's oxygen supply. If the flare-ups can't be tamed, remove the food until you regain control over the fire.

Direct-Heat Grilling with Charcoal

1 Light the coals as instructed on page 14.

2 After 15 to 20 minutes, the coals will be covered with gray ash and glowing. Remove the grill grate from the grill and pour the coals onto the fire bed.

3 With tongs, spread the coals in a single, snug layer, leaving a few cooler areas for dealing with flare-ups or food that is cooking too quickly. You can also create different heat levels by spreading the coals in a thick layer on one part of the fire bed, and a thinner layer on another part.

4 Place the grill grate on the grill and heat for a few minutes. Scrub the grate clean with a wire grill brush and oil it with a rolled-up paper towel dipped in oil.

5 Place the food directly over the fire and cook according to the recipe.

Indirect-Heat Grilling with Charcoal

1 Follow steps 1 and 2 for direct-heat grilling.

2 Arrange half the lit coals on one side of the fire bed and half on the other, leaving an area in the center free of coals. (Or, bank the lit coals to one side of the bed, leaving the other side free of coals.)

3 Put a drip pan (a disposable aluminum pan works well) in the space without coals. Place the grill grate on the grill, positioning it so that its handles are over the coals, and let it heat for a couple of minutes. Scrub the grate clean with a wire grill brush and oil it with a rolled-up paper towel dipped in oil.

4 Place the food on the grate over the drip pan, cover the grill, and adjust the vents as needed to reach the desired temperature. You can also use the direct-heat area of the grill to briefly sear the food, either before or after cooking it all the way through over the indirect-heat area.

5 The temperature of the fire should hold for about 2 hours (depending on what type of fuel you use, and how much). If the food needs to cook longer, add fresh briquettes or hardwood directly on the burning coals through the handles of the grill grate after about 1½ hours. Or, better yet, start more coals in the chimney starter and replenish the fire after about 2 hours.

Smoking with Charcoal

1 Soak the desired wood chips in cold or lukewarm water to cover for at least 30 minutes, wood chunks for at least 1 hour.

2 Light the coals as instructed on page 14.

3 After 15 to 20 minutes, the coals will be covered with gray ash and glowing. Remove the grill grate from the grill and pour the coals onto the fire bed.

4 Arrange half the lit coals on one side of the fire bed and half on the other, leaving an area in the center free of coals. (Or, bank the lit coals to one side of the bed, leaving the other side free of coals.)

5 Put a drip pan (a disposable aluminum pan works well) in the space without coals. Fill the drip pan with water or another liquid, like beer or apple juice, to create steam, which will help keep the food moist.

6 Add a handful (or the amount specified in a recipe) of drained chips or chunks to the coals. (You can also put the chips in the center of a large sheet of aluminum foil, fold to create a packet, and punch several holes in the foil to allow the smoke to escape. Place the packet directly on the coals.)

7 Place the grill grate on the grill, positioning it so that its handles are over the coals, and let it heat for a couple of minutes. Scrub the grate clean with a wire grill brush and oil it with a rolled-up paper towel dipped in oil.

8 Place the food on the grate over the drip pan, cover the grill, and adjust the vents until just barely open.

9 Add more wood chips every 30 minutes or so and wood chunks about every 45 minutes for at least the first 2 hours. Monitor the heat inside the grill, adding more briquettes or hardwood through the handles of the grill grate whenever the temperature starts to dip. If you're adding fresh briquettes or hardwood directly to the burning coals, you will probably need to add more every 1½ hours or so. If you're adding lit coals from the chimney starter, you should replenish the fire every 2 hours or so. Refill the drip pan with liquid as needed.

Grilling with Gas

Grilling with gas couldn't be easier, which makes a gas grill a good choice for folks with busy lives. The newest models have a slew of bells and whistles—warming rack, tool holder, side burner—and their boosters insist they turn out grilled foods with a flavor to rival their charcoal competition.

The Fuel Gas grills can operate on both natural gas and propane. Natural gas, which requires a small adjustment to the grill, is best for a stationary grill. Propane offers flexibility, but the tank must be replaced at regular intervals, which can be done at exchange stations at grocery, hardware, and home-improvement stores. A propane tank will usually give you about 15 hours of cooking time. Store it outside, away from direct sun and high temperatures. To avoid a "ran-out-of-fuel" disaster, keep an extra tank on hand.

Starting a Gas Grill Follow the instructions in the manual that came with your grill. It's typically as easy as opening the lid, turning on the gas, pushing the igniter button or striking a match, closing the lid, and letting the grill preheat. The final temperature needs to be at least 350° (180°C); 500° to 600°F (260° to 315°C) is even better.

Controlling the Heat Open the lid and adjust the temperature controls according to what you are cooking.

Direct-Heat Grilling with Gas

1 Ignite the grill, turn all the burners on to high, cover, and preheat for about 15 minutes, or a little longer in cool weather.

2 Open the lid and leave all the burners on. Scrub the grate clean with a wire grill brush and oil it with a rolled-up paper towel dipped in oil.

3 Adjust the controls to the heat level appropriate for the food you are cooking.

4 Place the food on the grate, and cook according to the recipe.

Indirect-Heat Grilling with Gas

1 Ignite the grill, turn all the burners on to high, cover, and preheat for about 15 minutes.

2 Open the lid and leave all the burners on. Scrub the grate clean with a wire grill brush and oil it with a rolled-up paper towel dipped in oil.

3 Depending on your burner setup, turn off the burner or burners that are directly under the area where the food will be placed. On two-burner models, this will be one burner; on three-burner models, this usually means the center burner. On larger grills, this can mean the center two or three burners. Most gas grills come equipped with a drip pan—if yours doesn't, place a drip pan underneath the area where the food will sit.

4 Place the food on the grate over the area without heat, cover the grill, and cook according to the recipe.

Smoking with Gas

1 Soak wood chips for at least 30 minutes, or chunks for at least 1 hour, then add some to the smoker box. (If your grill doesn't have a smoker box, you can make your own: place the chips in the center of a large sheet of aluminum foil, fold to create a compact packet, and punch several holes in the foil to allow the smoke to escape.) Place the box or packet on a burner, usually in the top left corner (check your grill manual). Place chunks at the back or on the sides of the grill grate.

2 Ignite the grill, turn all the burners on to high, cover, and preheat for about 15 minutes.

3 Open the lid and leave all the burners on. Scrub the grate clean with a wire grill brush and oil it with a rolled-up paper towel dipped in oil.

4 Cover the grill, and when you start to see smoke, after a few more minutes, set up the grill as directed in step 3 of indirect-heat grilling. Put a small pan of water or other liquid on the grate to create steam. Place the food on the grate over the area without heat, cover the grill, and cook according to the recipe.

5 Add more wood chips every 30 minutes or so and chunks every 45 minutes for at least the first 2 hours. Refill the pan with liquid as needed.

Safety and Grill Maintenance

Grilling, like all cooking, demands attention to safety, both for the fire and the food. And take care of your grill—a well-maintained grill will give you far fewer problems.

Grill Safety First, never set up your grill in an enclosed space or under an overhang. Once the grill is lit, don't leave it unattended, try to move it, or let curious kids or pets get too close. When you have finished cooking on a charcoal grill, cover it and close the vents to put out the fire. For a gas grill, turn off the fuel at the source.

Food Safety Follow your usual kitchen rules, such as clean hands and equipment, and thaw any frozen food in the refrigerator, not at room temperature. Here are a few more guidelines: Don't leave food at room temperature longer than 2 hours, or 1 hour in hot weather, and never put cooked food on a platter that held raw food without washing the platter first. If a sauce will be used for both basting and at the table, divide it before you begin basting, and if you are basting with a marinade that was used for raw food, boil it for 2 minutes before using, or stop basting at least 5 minutes before the food is removed from the grill.

Caring for Your Grill Some folks think that maintaining a grill must be a lot of work, but it isn't. That said, you can't let the maintenance slide, or your grill will be a sluggish performer. If you have a new grill, check the manual that came with it for any special instructions before you use it. Below are some general rules that apply to all grills:

- Before anything goes on the grill grate, brush it with oil. This prevents the food from sticking and it speeds cleanup.

- Just as important, when the food comes off the grill and the grate is still hot, use a long-handled wire brush to dislodge any food stuck to the bars.

- Once a charcoal grill has cooled completely and the ashes are dead cold, shovel them out into a nonflammable container and discard them. Ashes are acidic, and that acidity can weaken the bottom of the grill.

- If you have a gas grill, clean the gas jets often by scraping or brushing the jets in the direction that the gas flows, not back toward you. If your gas grill has lava rocks or ceramic briquettes, sort through them occasionally and remove any food scraps. If they are heavily soiled, replace them with new rocks or briquettes.

- Every now and again, rinse the outside of the grill with soapy water. If you have the room, move your grill indoors when you are not using it or slip a weather-resistant cover over the grill.

Is It Done Yet?

Using an instant-read thermometer is the most accurate way to judge the doneness of a large piece of meat. Be sure to insert the tip of the thermometer into the center of the meat, away from any bone or fatty areas. Also, remember that the internal temperature of the meat will rise 5° to 10°F (3° to 6°C) after you remove it from the heat and let it rest. The chart to the right gives temperatures for when I'd suggest taking the meat off the grill, before resting.

The easiest way to test smaller cuts of meat—like burgers, steaks, chops, and pork tenderloins—for doneness is by poking them with your index finger. Professional cooks use this method, and it's pretty darn accurate once you get the hang of it. Follow my touch test and you'll be on the right track:

Rare Meat feels like your cheek.

Medium-Rare Meat feels like the tip of your nose.

Medium Meat feels just slightly firmer than the tip of your nose.

Well Done Meat feels like your forehead.

RED MEAT

BURGERS	**145°F (63°C)** for rare to medium-rare	Feels like the tip of your nose; pink and juicy interior
	150°F (65°C) for medium	Feels slightly firmer than the tip of your nose; pink only at center
	160°F (71°C) for medium-well to well done	Feels like your forehead; no traces of pink remain
STEAKS AND LAMB CHOPS	**125°–135°F (52°–57°C)** for rare to medium-rare	Feels like your cheek; rosy-pink interior
	140°F (60°C) for medium	Feels like the tip of your nose; pink only at center
	150°–160°F (65°–71°C) for medium-well to well done	Feels like your forehead; no traces of pink remain
BEEF AND LAMB ROASTS	**125°–135°F (52°–57°C)** for rare to medium-rare	Feels like your cheek; rosy-pink interior
	140°F (60°C) for medium	Feels like the tip of your nose; pink only at center
	150°–160°F (65°–71°C) for medium-well to well done	Feels like your forehead; no traces of pink remain

PORK

CHOPS AND TENDERLOINS	**145°F (63°C)** for medium	Feels slightly firmer than the tip of your nose; pink only at center
	150°–160°F (65°–71°C) for medium-well to well done	Feels like your forehead; no traces of pink remain
ROASTS	**145°F (63°C)** for medium	Feels slightly firmer than the tip of your nose; pink only at center
	150°–160°F (65°–71°C) for medium-well to well done	Feels like your forehead; no traces of pink remain
RIBS	**150°–160°F (65°–71°C)**	Ribs bend without resistance; meat pulls easily from the bone

POULTRY

WHOLE CHICKENS	**165°–170°F (74°–77°C)**	Juices run clear when a thigh joint is pierced
BONELESS CHICKEN BREASTS	**160°F (71°C)**	Feels firm to the touch; meat is opaque
DRUMSTICKS, THIGHS, AND WINGS	**170°F (77°C)**	Feels firm to the touch; meat releases easily from the bone
BONELESS DUCK BREASTS	**135°–140°F (52°–60°C)**	Feels slightly firm to the touch; meat is pinkish red
BONE-IN TURKEY BREASTS	**165°F (74°C)**	Feels firm to the touch; meat is opaque

The Raw Ingredients

What goes on the grill should be the best your budget allows. Grilling tends to intensify the natural flavors of whatever is being cooked, so if you buy great stuff, it will taste great at the table. Here are some tips on what to look for at the butcher shop.

Red Meat The best beef and lamb have bright red, fine-textured flesh, light, evenly distributed marbling, and nearly white exterior fat. Instead of grilling the same steak every time, experiment with different cuts—you'll be pleasantly surprised.

- Among the best beef steak choices for the grill are T-bone, New York strip, porterhouse, and rib eye. They cook quickly, taste great, and need little adornment.

- Top sirloin steaks are tasty and offer a good value; they are also my top choice for kebabs. Tri-tip, a triangular cut from the bottom of the sirloin, is awesome for a crowd.

- Flank, skirt, and hanger steaks are chewier and benefit from an overnight marinade, but don't let that dissuade you from buying them. They'll shine in tacos, sandwiches, and salads.

- Never hesitate to cook a prime rib roast, whole beef tenderloin, beef ribs, or leg of lamb on the grill over indirect heat: the result is stunning.

Pork Look for pork that is well trimmed, reddish pink, and free of dark patches. Pork and the grill were made for each other, so don't ignore this section of the meat counter.

- Bone-in loin and rib chops are a great change from steak.

- Try out different types of sausages on the grill. Bratwurst and andouille are two of my favorites.

- Pork tenderloins are quick cooking enough for every day and elegant enough for special occasions.

- The shoulder and ham make awesome 'cue, and ribs, of course, are nearly everyone's favorite.

Poultry Poultry, both whole birds and parts, should be evenly colored—white to pale yellow—and any visible fat should be pale yellow. Look for plump whole birds with firm flesh. Explore the world of grilled poultry beyond the boneless chicken breast.

- Mixed chicken parts—wings, breasts, thighs—go well with almost any sauce, glaze, or marinade, plus, everyone can pick their favorite part.

- Roasting a whole chicken on the grill is easier than you think. Put the bird right on the grill grate, or use a beer can to stand it up (see page 128).

- Boneless duck breasts take to grilling, with their skin developing a tasty golden char.

Getting to Know Your Butcher

Butchers, whether at a grocery store or meat market, are good people to be friends with. Most butchers will grind meat to your specification, carve large cuts into manageable pieces, trim a beef tenderloin, and even butterfly a chicken. When you need something special, give your butcher advance notice, and he or she will probably be glad to do it.

Freezing and Thawing

To freeze meat or poultry, wrap in plastic wrap or aluminum foil, slip into a lock-top plastic freezer bag, and seal closed, pressing out as much air from the bag as possible. Even better, use a vacuum sealer to wrap meat or poultry for freezing. Label and date the package and freeze for no more than 9 months (4 months for ground meat). Always thaw frozen items in the refrigerator, allowing 2 days for most foods. In a pinch, you can use a cold-water bath to thaw more quickly.

Reading the Label

Nowadays, we see all kinds of labels on meat and poultry: all-natural, free-range, grass-fed, hormone-free, organic. They are attached to what I call "pasture-perfect proteins," which typically taste better than conventionally raised meat and poultry. My advice is try them out on your grill. Note that free-range and organic chickens cook faster than non-organic birds.

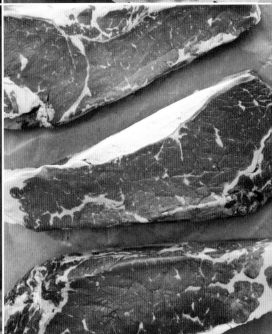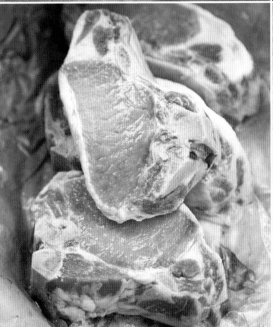

Grilling Dos

1. Make sure you understand the difference between direct-heat and indirect-heat grilling (page 12), and when you should use each method.

2. Always let the grill preheat fully. If you put the food on too soon, it won't cook right.

3. Keep the grill grate clean. Otherwise, the food will stick and taste like last week's grilled supper.

4. Oil the grill grate. The oil prevents the food from sticking and helps transfer the heat more quickly. And except for fattier foods, you should oil the food, too.

5. In general, cook with the grill lid on, even for direct-heat grilling. One exception is tuna steaks, which can easily go from wonderful to "whoops" in a covered grill.

6. Leave food directly over a hot fire long enough for the surface to caramelize, but not so long that it blackens, which will heighten its flavor.

7. Turn foods only once, if possible. They will cook more evenly and are less likely to buckle and break.

8. Use a thermometer to gauge both the grill temperature and the internal food temperature of larger cuts of meat.

9. Let meats and poultry rest before serving, to allow their juices to redistribute evenly, ensuring juiciness and better flavor.

10. Follow the maintenance schedule detailed in the grill's manual. It will make your life easier and your grill's life longer.

Grilling Don'ts

1. Never rush. Grilling is a little Zen-like. When you rush, you make mistakes.

2. Don't skimp on the ingredients. Grilling highlights the natural flavors of foods, and cheap food will taste like it.

3. Don't cut into meat or poultry to check for doneness. All the delicious juices will run right out. Instead, spring for an instant-read thermometer or master the touch test (see page 20).

4. Don't get caught without an extra bag of charcoal or an extra propane tank. Almost nothing is worse than running out of fuel with a half-cooked bird on the grate.

5. Avoid briquettes infused with starter fluid. The fluid can impart an unpleasant taste to whatever you are grilling.

6. Don't throw a steak straight from the fridge onto a hot grill. Bring foods to room temperature to ensure they cook evenly.

7. Once your coals are lit, don't put the hot chimney starter on or near anything that's flammable, like your grass lawn.

8. It's always fun to visit with guests, but not when they are far away from the grill. Don't get distracted, or you might end up with cinders instead of kebabs.

9. When cooking directly over the fire, never use a basting sauce that contains sugar until the last 10 minutes of grilling. Basting earlier will result in crusty, singed food that you cannot resurrect.

10. Loose clothes and swinging hair have no place around an open fire. Tuck in your shirt, tie back your hair if it's long, and forget the muumuu.

How to grill the perfect
Cheeseburger

The cheeseburger is an American culinary icon, and anyone who fires up a grill needs a recipe that honors that status. A good cheeseburger is a pleasure, but a great cheeseburger is an experience, and these tips will show you how to make the best.

CHOOSE THE BEST MEAT The fat-to-lean ratio of the meat is critical for a juicy burger. After decades of testing, I have found that equal parts ground chuck and ground sirloin consistently deliver the best balance of flavor and fat. If you want a deeper, richer, beefier flavor, buy grass-fed beef.

MAKE GOOD-SIZED PATTIES Gently shape the meat into patties just until they hold together, and make them thick enough so they will pick up a grill flavor without overcooking. My burgers usually weigh about ⅓ pound (155 g) and are 1 inch (2.5 cm) thick.

PREVENT A "SWOLLEN BELLY" Make an indentation in the center of each patty with your thumb. This prevents what I call the swollen-belly syndrome: burgers that are not as juicy as they should be and are puffed up and smaller than you intended.

COOL DOWN THE PATTIES Chill your patties in the refrigerator—a half hour is good, and an hour is even better—before you grill them. They will hold together better over the fire and cook more evenly.

GET THE FIRE HOT A burger picks up caramelized flavor when it hits a sizzling-hot grill, so I start with a hot fire. You can always adjust the heat afterward.

DON'T PRESS Never press down on a burger with a spatula when it is on the grill. All that does is push out the flavorful juices.

TOAST THE BUNS Give the buns a quick toasting on the grill—this simple step will help boost the burgers' quality by a mile.

DON'T OVERDO THE CONDIMENTS Let the cheese and the burger shine. I dress my cheeseburger with a little mayonnaise (I'm southern), a tomato slice, and thinly sliced onions, which I caramelize if I have the time.

Cheeseburgers

1 lb (500 g) *each* ground chuck
and ground sirloin

Kosher salt and freshly ground pepper

6 slices of your favorite cheese

6 hamburger buns, split

Ripe tomato slices; crisp lettuce leaves;
red onion slices; bread-and-butter
or dill pickle slices; and mayonnaise,
mustard, and ketchup, for serving

---

1 Prepare a charcoal or gas grill for direct grilling over high heat (page 16 or 18). Brush and oil the grill grate.

2 In a large bowl, using a spoon, not your hands, gently mix together the chuck and sirloin. Run your hands under cold water and then divide the mixture into 6 equal portions. Shape each portion into a patty about 1 inch (2.5 cm) thick, being careful not to compact the meat too much. (Check to make sure the patties fit the buns, too.) Season on both sides with salt and pepper. Make a depression in the center of each patty with your thumb. Refrigerate until the grill is ready.

3 Place the patties, indent side up, on the grill directly over the fire and cook, turning once, until they are nicely charred on both sides, 4–5 minutes per side for medium. During the last 2 minutes of cooking, place a cheese slice on each patty and put the buns, cut side down, along the edge of the grill, then cover the grill. After about 2 minutes, the cheese should be melted and the buns toasted.

4 Place the burgers on the bun bottoms and place the tops alongside. Set out the condiments for diners to add as desired. Serve at once.

SERVES 6

Patty Melts
with Charred Onions

1 lb (500 g) ground chuck

1 lb (500 g) ground sirloin

Kosher salt and freshly ground pepper

12 slices rye bread

6 tablespoons (3 oz/90 g) unsalted butter, melted

2 sweet onions, thickly sliced

6 slices good-quality Swiss cheese such as Gruyère or Comté

SERVES 6

The Game Plan

- Set up grill for direct grilling over high heat

- Shape meat into patties; refrigerate until ready to grill

- Slice onions and cheese

- Melt butter then brush onto bread slices

- Grilling time: 8–10 minutes

- DON'T FORGET Try to shape the burger patties to fit the bread slices, but don't handle the meat too much (they don't have to be perfect).

This is one of my favorite burgers. The charred onions develop a deep sweetness that perfectly counterbalances the earthy, slightly sour character of the rye bread and the nutty flavor of the Swiss cheese. This is a first-class knife-and-fork burger that you will want to eat again and again.

1 Prepare a charcoal or gas grill for direct grilling over high heat (page 16 or 18). Brush and oil the grill grate.

2 In a large bowl, using a spoon, not your hands, gently mix together the chuck and sirloin. Run your hands under cold water and divide the mixture into 6 equal portions. Shape each portion into a patty about the size and shape of a slice of bread, being careful not to compact the meat too much. Season on both sides with salt and pepper. Make a depression in the center of each patty with your thumb. Refrigerate the patties until the grill is ready.

3 Brush both sides of each bread slice with the butter.

4 Place the patties, indent side up, and onion slices on the grill directly over the fire. Cook, turning once, until both the patties and the onions are nicely charred on both sides and the burgers are cooked to your liking, 4–5 minutes per side for medium. During the last 2 minutes of cooking, top each patty with a slice of cheese and put the bread slices along the edge of the grill, then cover the grill. Grill, turning the bread slices once, until the cheese is melted and the bread is lightly toasted.

5 Place each burger on a slice of toasted rye. Toss the onion slices to break up the rings, and divide evenly among the burgers. Top each burger with a second slice of toasted bread and serve at once.

GOES GREAT WITH Smoky Grilled Potatoes (page 176); Mac and Cheese (page 196); Watermelon Salad (page 203)

Jalapeño-Bacon-Cheddar Burgers

1 lb (500 g) ground chuck

1 lb (500 g) ground sirloin

Kosher salt and freshly
ground pepper

6 jalapeño chiles, stemmed,
halved lengthwise, and seeded

6 slices Cheddar cheese

12 slices thick-cut applewood-
smoked bacon, fried until crisp

6 hamburger buns, split

Classic BBQ Sauce (page 212),
or your favorite BBQ sauce,
for serving

Lettuce, tomato slices, and
onion slices for serving
(optional)

SERVES 6

The Game Plan

- Set up grill for direct grilling
  over high heat

- Shape meat into patties;
  refrigerate until ready to grill

- Cook bacon, prepare chiles,
  and slice cheese

- Grilling time: 8–10 minutes

- DON'T FORGET The jalapeño
  halves can easily slip through
  the grill grate, so be careful
  as you turn them, or use a
  grill basket.

Although you may think this burger looks too spicy, it's not. The
Cheddar and bacon tame the jalapeños so that they deliver just
enough fire to satisfy, rather than scorch. Quality ingredients make
the difference here, so buy first-rate Cheddar and applewood-
smoked bacon. In a pinch, you can use pickled jalapeños, but
you'll miss the delicious smokiness the grill imparts to fresh chiles.

1 Prepare a charcoal or gas grill for direct grilling over high heat (page 16
or 18). Brush and oil the grill grate.

2 In a bowl, using a spoon, not your hands, gently mix together the chuck
and sirloin. Run your hands under cold water and then divide the mixture
into 6 equal portions. Shape each portion into a patty about 1 inch (2.5 cm)
thick, being careful not to compact the meat too much. (Check to make sure
the patties fit the buns, too.) Season on both sides with salt and pepper. Make
a depression in the center of each patty with your thumb. Refrigerate the
patties until the grill is ready.

3 Place the patties, indent side up, and the chiles, skin side down, on the
grill directly over the fire. Grill both the patties and the chiles, turning once,
until they are nicely charred on both sides and the burgers are cooked to your
liking, 4–5 minutes per side for medium. During the last 2 minutes of cooking,
top each patty with a cheese slice, 2 chile halves, and 2 bacon slices. Put the
buns, cut side down, along the edge of the grill and cover the grill. Grill until
the cheese is melted and the buns are lightly toasted.

4 Place the burgers on the bun bottoms and place the tops alongside. Set
out the BBQ sauce and other accompaniments, if desired, for diners to add
to their burgers. Serve at once.

GOES GREAT WITH Smoky Baked Beans with Bacon (page 194); Potato Salad
(page 195); Creamy Coleslaw (page 202)

Lamb Burgers
with Mint-Feta Pesto

2 tablespoons finely chopped shallot

2 tablespoons finely chopped fresh flat-leaf parsley

1 tablespoon finely chopped fresh mint

1 tablespoon Dijon mustard

2 teaspoons dried rosemary, crushed

1 clove garlic, minced

1½ lb (750 g) ground lamb

½ lb (250 g) ground beef chuck

Kosher salt and freshly ground pepper

6 pita rounds

Mint-Feta Pesto (page 214) for serving

Shredded lettuce for serving

SERVES 6

The Game Plan

- Make mint-feta pesto; refrigerate

- Set up grill for direct grilling over high heat

- Season meat and shape into patties; shred lettuce

- Grilling time: about 10 minutes

- DON'T FORGET Some folks like lamb burgers more rare than others: I suggest asking diners before grilling.

The smell of lamb burgers cooking over a hot fire is intoxicating. In fact, the aroma is so wonderful that even if I've just finished eating, it makes me want to eat more. Add a little feta-laced mint pesto and some lightly toasted pita bread, and you've got a pretty nice Greek meal on the table.

1 Prepare a charcoal or gas grill for direct grilling over high heat (page 16 or 18). Brush and oil the grill grate.

2 In a bowl, mix together the shallot, parsley, mint, mustard, rosemary, and garlic. Gently work in the lamb and beef until well blended. A tablespoon or two of ice water sometimes helps with the mixing. Divide the meat mixture into 6 equal portions. Shape each portion into a patty about 1 inch (2.5 cm) thick, being careful not to compact the meat too much. Season on both sides with salt and pepper. Make a depression in the center of each patty with your thumb.

3 Place the patties, indent side up, on the grill directly over the fire and cook, turning once, until nicely charred on both sides, about 5 minutes per side for medium. The patty should give slightly when pressed. During the last 2 minutes of cooking, throw the pitas onto the edge of the grill and toast lightly, turning once.

4 Transfer the burgers to a platter. Cut off and discard about one-third of each pita round and open up the pocket. Place a little of the mint-feta pesto in the bottom of each pita, add a lamb burger, and top with shredded lettuce and a little more pesto. Serve at once.

GOES GREAT WITH Grilled Eggplant with Feta (page 172); Herbed Rice Pilaf (page 197); Greek Salad (page 205)

Southwestern Buffalo Burgers

FOR THE CHIPOTLE MAYO

1 cup (8 fl oz/250 ml)
mayonnaise, preferably
homemade (page 216)

1 chipotle chile in adobo
sauce, chopped

2 tablespoons chopped
fresh cilantro

Juice from ¼ lime

Kosher salt and freshly
ground pepper

2 lb (1 kg) ground buffalo

½ cup (4 oz/125 g) chopped
roasted green chiles, jarred or
thawed frozen

6 slices Monterey jack cheese

6 kaiser rolls, split

6 thick tomato slices (optional)

SERVES 6

The Game Plan

- Make chipotle mayo;
  refrigerate
- Set up grill for direct grilling
  over high heat
- Shape meat into patties;
  refrigerate until ready to grill
- Grilling time: about
  10 minutes
- DON'T FORGET Have the
  chiles and cheese ready so
  you can throw them on the
  patties at the right time.

Over the past few years, I have often visited New Mexico, where the green chile cheeseburger reigns supreme. The state even has its own Green Chile Cheeseburger Trail, so you know there's some great eating there. This recipe honors that tradition, even though it departs from it with ground buffalo instead of beef and chipotle mayonnaise along with fresh green chiles.

1 To make the chipotle mayo, in a bowl, stir together the mayonnaise, chipotle chile, cilantro, and lime juice. Season with salt and pepper. (The mayo can be made up to 1 week in advance and refrigerated.)

2 Prepare a charcoal or gas grill for direct grilling over high heat (page 16 or 18). Brush and oil the grill grate.

3 Divide the meat into 6 equal portions. Shape each portion into a patty about 1 inch (2.5 cm) thick, being careful not to compact the meat too much. Season on both sides with salt and pepper. Make a depression in the center of each patty with your thumb. Refrigerate the patties until the grill is ready.

4 Place the patties, indent side up, on the grill directly over the fire and cook until nicely charred on both sides, about 5 minutes per side. During the last 2 minutes of cooking, divide the green chiles evenly among the patties, arranging them on top, and then top each patty with a slice of cheese. Place the rolls, cut side down, along the edge of the grill and cover the grill. Grill until the cheese is melted and the rolls are lightly toasted.

5 Place the burgers on the roll bottoms and place the tops alongside. Serve with the chipotle mayo and the tomato slices, if desired.

GOES GREAT WITH Grilled Corn with Lime Butter (page 165); Southwestern Bean Salad (page 195); Tortilla chips and Creamy Avocado Salsa (page 215)

Smoky Chili Dogs

FOR THE CHILI

1 lb (500 g) lean ground beef

1 cup (8 oz/250 g) ketchup

2 chipotle chiles in adobo sauce, finely chopped

1 tablespoon sugar

1 tablespoon chile powder

1 tablespoon cider vinegar

1 bay leaf

Kosher salt and freshly ground pepper

8 hot dogs, preferably kosher beef

8 hot dog buns

Shredded Cheddar cheese and chopped white onion for serving

SERVES 8

The Game Plan

- Make chili; keep warm or reheat before serving

- Set up grill for direct grilling over high heat

- Shred cheese and chop onion

- Grilling time: 5–10 minutes

- DON'T FORGET Keep a close watch on the hot dogs as they grill—even this delicious chili won't mask the taste of burnt dogs.

Every part of the country has its own hot dog tradition. Some dogs are garlicky, some are deep red, some are long and skinny, and some are short and stout. But no matter what kind of hot dogs folks favor, they always taste better grilled. Add a big spoonful of smoky chili and a grill-toasted bun to these hefty beef dogs, and you'll make your own new tradition.

1 To make the chili, in a large frying pan over medium heat, cook the ground beef, breaking up any large clumps, until browned, about 3 minutes. Add ¼ cup (2 fl oz/60 ml) water and break up the beef a bit more. Stir in the ketchup, chiles, sugar, chile powder, vinegar, and bay leaf, mixing well. Simmer, uncovered, until thickened to a nice chili consistency, about 30 minutes. Season with salt and pepper. Remove and discard the bay leaf. Remove the chili from the heat and cover to keep warm. (The chili can be made in advance, tightly covered, and refrigerated for up to 4 days or frozen for up to 3 months. Reheat before serving.)

2 Prepare a charcoal or gas grill for direct grilling over high heat (page 16 or 18). Brush and oil the grill grate.

3 Place the hot dogs on the grill directly over the fire and cook, rolling the hot dogs every few minutes, until heated through, about 5 minutes. Then ask the guests how they like their hot dogs. Some will want them burnt and puffy, some will want them a little blackened, and some will want them exactly the way they are right now. Remove the hot dogs according to the answers you get. Place the buns, cut side down, along the edge of the grill and grill for a minute or two until toasted.

4 Place a hot dog in each bun and top with the chili, cheese, and onions. Serve at once.

GOES GREAT WITH Potato Salad (page 195); Creamy Coleslaw (page 202); Chopped Salad (page 204)

How to grill the perfect
Steak

Aside from burgers and hot dogs, steaks hit the grill more often than just about anything else. I grew up eating a grilled steak every Saturday night, and sitting down to a good steak once a week is still part of my routine. Why? Because it's just doggone good eating. Here are some tips on how to cook the perfect grilled steak.

BUY GOOD MEAT Grass-fed and grass-finished beef tastes better and has a bolder flavor that holds up particularly well against the lick of the grill's flames.

SIMPLE SEASONING I sprinkle steak liberally on both sides with salt and pepper when I take it out of the refrigerator, which seems to help it form a nice crust over the fire. Chefs have different opinions about salting. Some salt a steak the night before, some after the steak is cooked. I have tried both, and I find that my way still works best. I also like to brush steaks on both sides with a little olive oil (not extra virgin). This facilitates the heat transfer, so you get an evenly browned crust and a delicious steak house flavor.

TIMING IS IMPORTANT There's nothing worse than a rubbery, tasteless, overcooked steak. Professionals use touch to gauge doneness, and so can you. Touch your index finger to your cheek. When the meat feels this way, the steak is rare. Touch the tip of your nose. That firmness equates to medium. Your forehead is well done. But please don't go there.

LET IT REST If you cut into a piece of beef as soon as it comes off the grill, you will lose precious juices. Give the proteins in the steak the opportunity to unwind a little bit from the heat they have just experienced. Let most steaks rest for at least 5 minutes—10 minutes is even better—to give the juices time to redistribute evenly throughout the meat.

GOES GREAT WITH Skip the steak sauce—a pat of plain or compound butter (like the black-pepper butter in this recipe) is the perfect finish. Some great sides: Chopped Salad (page 204), Grilled Asparagus with Lemon Mayonnaise (page 166), and The Best Mashed Potatoes (page 198).

T-Bone Steaks
with Black-Pepper Butter

FOR THE BLACK-PEPPER BUTTER

½ cup (4 oz/125 g) unsalted butter, at room temperature

2 tablespoons chopped shallots

1 tablespoon cracked pepper

1 teaspoon steak sauce

Kosher salt

6 T-bone steaks, each about 10 oz (315 g) and 1½ inches (4 cm) thick

Kosher salt and freshly ground pepper

6 tablespoons (3 fl oz/90 ml) olive oil

1 To make the black-pepper butter, place the butter in a small bowl. Using a fork, work in the shallots, pepper, and steak sauce, distributing them evenly. Season with salt. Transfer to an airtight container and refrigerate to harden. Or, if you want to get fancy, spoon the butter into a rough log shape near one long edge of a 12-by-6-inch (30-by-15-cm) sheet of waxed paper. Roll the paper over the butter, and press the butter into a solid, uniform log. Continue rolling the waxed paper around the butter, and twist both ends to seal securely, then refrigerate. (The butter will keep refrigerated for up to 1 week or frozen for up to 1 month.)

2 At least 30 minutes before you are ready to begin grilling, remove the steaks from the refrigerator. Season the steaks generously on both sides with salt and pepper.

3 Prepare a charcoal or gas grill for direct grilling over high heat (page 16 or 18). Brush and oil the grill grate.

4 Brush the steaks on both sides with the oil. Place the steaks on the grill directly over the fire, and cook for about 3 minutes. Using tongs or a wide spatula, rotate each steak a quarter turn (90 degrees). This will give you those beautiful crisscrossed grill marks that will impress your neighbors. Continue cooking for another 2–3 minutes, then turn the steaks. Cook until well marked and done to your liking, another 5 minutes for medium-rare, or until an instant-read thermometer inserted horizontally into the center of a steak away from bone registers 135°F (57°C).

5 Transfer the steaks to warmed plates. Put a healthy pat of the butter on each steak and let the steaks rest for 5–10 minutes. Serve to oohs and aahs.

SERVES 6

Cowboy Rib Eyes
with Charred Corn and Tomato Salad

3 tablespoons *each* Dijon mustard and cider vinegar

Juice of ½ lemon

1 teaspoon *each* chopped garlic and chopped shallot

½ teaspoon sugar

¼ teaspoon cracked yellow mustard seeds

½ cup (4 fl oz/125 ml) olive oil

4 bone-in rib-eye steaks, preferably long bone, each about 1½ inches (4 cm) thick

Chipotle Spice Paste (page 209)

4 ears corn, preferably yellow, shucked

1 cup (6 oz/185 g) cherry tomatoes, halved

2 tablespoons chopped fresh basil

SERVES 4

The Game Plan

- Make salad dressing and spice paste

- Remove steaks from fridge and coat with spice paste

- Set up grill for direct grilling over 2 heat levels: high and medium-high

- Grilling time: 5–7 minutes for corn; 12 minutes for steaks

- DON'T FORGET Rotate the steaks 90 degrees every few minutes to get grill marks.

This is the perfect midsummer cookout fare when corn is at its peak and tomatoes are bursting and luscious. If possible, get bone-in rib eyes, and if you have a good butcher, ask for the long-bone cut, aka the cowboy or tomahawk steak. The chipotle spice paste adds tons of flavor to the beef and pairs nicely with a corn and cherry tomato salad.

1 To make the dressing for the salad, in a blender or food processor, combine the mustard, vinegar, lemon juice, garlic, shallot, sugar, and mustard seeds. Pulse briefly to mix. With the motor running, slowly add the oil and process until the mixture emulsifies. Set aside until ready to use.

2 At least 30 minutes before you are ready to begin grilling, remove the steaks from the refrigerator. Rub the spice paste over both sides of the steaks.

3 Prepare a charcoal or gas grill for direct grilling over two levels of heat, one high and one medium-high (page 16 or 18). Brush and oil the grill grate.

4 Place the corn on the grill over the medium-high zone and cook, turning every couple of minutes, until they are lightly charred all the way around and the kernels are tender, 5–7 minutes. Let cool while you grill the steaks.

5 Place the steaks on the hottest part of the grill and cook for 4 minutes. Using tongs or a wide spatula, rotate each steak a quarter turn (90 degrees), and continue cooking for another 3 minutes, then turn the steaks. Cook the steaks until well marked and cooked to your liking, about another 5 minutes for medium-rare, or until an instant-read thermometer inserted into the center of a steak away from the bone registers 135°F (57°C). If you want to cook the steaks to medium, find a cool spot along the edge of your charcoal grill or cut the burners down on your gas grill to medium heat.

6 Transfer the steaks to warmed plates and let rest for 5–10 minutes. Holding each ear of corn stem end down on a board, cut off the kernels with a sharp knife. Transfer the kernels to a bowl. Pour the mustard dressing over the corn, add the tomatoes and basil, and toss well. Serve the steaks at once and pass the salad at the table.

GOES GREAT WITH Smoky Grilled Potatoes (page 176); Drunken Pinto Beans (page 194); Mexican Rice (page 197)

New York Strip Steaks
with Bourbon Steak Sauce

4 bone-in New York strip steaks, each about 10 oz (315 g) and 1½ inches (4 cm) thick

½ cup (4 oz/125 g) unsalted butter, melted and cooled

¼ cup (2 fl oz/60 ml) canola oil

Kosher salt and freshly ground pepper

Bourbon Steak Sauce (page 213) for serving

SERVES 4

The Game Plan

- Make steak sauce; refrigerate

- Melt and cool butter; combine with oil

- Remove steaks from fridge; coat with oil-butter mixture and season

- Set up grill for direct grilling over high heat

- Grilling time: about 12 minutes

- DON'T FORGET The oil-butter mixture promotes browning and gives the steaks great flavor—don't skip this step.

The New York strip is my absolute favorite steak. And because I am a southerner, bourbon has been known to touch my lips. Combine the two and you come up with this elegant yet easy grilled main course. Don't be tempted to take a shortcut and just add bourbon to commercial steak sauce. This sauce is far better than anything you can buy in a store.

1 At least 30 minutes before you are ready to begin grilling, remove the steaks from the refrigerator. In a 9-by-13-inch (23-by-33-cm) baking dish, mix together the butter and oil. Place the steaks in the mixture and turn to coat both sides. One at a time, lift the steaks from the dish, allow the excess oil mixture to drip back into the dish, and place on a platter. Coat each steak on both sides with 1 teaspoon each salt and pepper.

2 Prepare a charcoal or gas grill for direct grilling over high heat (page 16 or 18). Brush and oil the grill grate.

3 Place the steaks on the grill directly over the fire and cook for about 3 minutes. Using tongs or a wide spatula, rotate each steak a quarter turn (90 degrees), and continue cooking for another 3 minutes, then turn the steaks. Cook the steaks until well marked and cooked to your liking, about another 5 minutes for medium-rare, or until an instant-read thermometer inserted into the center of a steak away from bone registers 135°F (57°C). If you want to cook the steaks to medium, find a cool spot along the edge of your charcoal grill or cut the burners down on your gas grill to medium heat.

4 Transfer the steaks to warmed plates and let rest for 5–10 minutes. Serve at once. Pass the steak sauce at the table.

GOES GREAT WITH Creamed Spinach (page 198); Grilled Veggies (page 201); Spinach and Bacon Salad (page 205)

Classic Beef Kebabs

Rosemary-Lemon Marinade
(page 210)

1 lb (500 g) top sirloin, cut into
1-inch (2.5-cm) cubes

12 cremini mushrooms

2 small red onions, each cut
into 6 wedges

1 zucchini, halved lengthwise
and cut into 12 half-moons

2 tablespoons canola oil

Kosher salt and freshly
ground pepper

6–12 metal or wooden skewers

SERVES 6

The Game Plan

- Make marinade; reserve
  some for brushing

- Cube beef; marinate for
  1 hour or up to overnight

- Remove beef from fridge
  and discard marinade; soak
  skewers if using wooden

- Cut vegetables; toss with oil

- Set up grill for direct grilling
  over high heat

- Skewer beef and vegetables

- Grilling time: 6–8 minutes

- Brush with reserved marinade
  during grilling

- DON'T FORGET These will
  cook quickly; if they start
  to char too soon, move
  them to a cooler area
  of the grill (or lower the
  heat if using gas).

The kebab is probably where grilling started. Think about it: a stick, some meat, a fire. I've elevated the form here with a rosemary-infused marinade and a trio of vegetables. I typically load up an extra skewer of vegetables because it's easy to do and diners are always happy to have a few extra grilled veggies on their plates.

1 Measure and set aside ¼ cup (2 fl oz/60 ml) of the marinade. Place the beef cubes in a large lock-top plastic bag and pour in the remaining marinade. Seal the bag closed, squish the marinade around the meat, and marinate at room temperature for at least 1 hour, or preferably overnight in the refrigerator.

2 At least 30 minutes before you are ready to begin grilling, remove the beef from the refrigerator. Discard the marinade. In a medium bowl, toss the mushrooms, onions, and zucchini with the oil, then season with salt and pepper. If using wooden skewers, soak them in water for at least 30 minutes.

3 Prepare a charcoal or gas grill for direct grilling over high heat (page 16 or 18). Brush and oil the grill grate.

4 Thread the beef and vegetables onto the skewers, dividing them evenly and starting and ending with a cube of meat, until the skewer is full. Thread any leftover vegetables onto a separate skewer.

5 Place the skewers on the grill directly over the fire and brush with some of the reserved marinade. Cook for 3–4 minutes, then turn the skewers and brush with more marinade. (Tongs are perfect for turning the kebabs.) Continue cooking for another 3–4 minutes for medium-rare. The vegetables should be cooked but firm, and the meat should give easily when pressed.

6 Brush the skewers with the marinade a final time, then transfer to a platter and let rest for about 5 minutes. Slide the beef and vegetables off the skewers onto the platter and serve at once.

GOES GREAT WITH Herbed Rice Pilaf (page 197); Greek Salad (page 205); Garlic Bread (page 207)

Bacon-Wrapped Filets Mignons
with Simple Béarnaise Sauce

8 slices thick-cut applewood-smoked bacon

4 filets mignons, each about 10 oz (315 g) and 1½ inches (4 cm) thick

Kosher salt and freshly ground pepper

Canola oil for brushing

Simple Béarnaise Sauce (page 216), warmed, for serving

SERVES 4

The Game Plan

- Make béarnaise sauce; keep warm

- Blanch bacon; drain

- Wrap bacon around steaks and secure with string

- Season steaks and brush with oil

- Set up grill for direct grilling over high heat

- Grilling time: about 12 minutes

- DON'T FORGET Be sure to buy filets that are at least 1½ inches (4 cm) thick, to accommodate the bacon.

The filet mignon, dubbed the King of Steak, is relatively lean and extremely tender but sometimes needs a little flavor help. Bacon delivers that help here. I blanch the bacon slices first so they will be nice and crisp when the steaks are done. Even though I have simplified the béarnaise sauce, it has the smooth, velvety character of the classic.

1 Bring a saucepan half full of water to a boil over high heat. Add the bacon, reduce the heat to medium, and cook for 5 minutes. Using a slotted spoon, transfer the bacon to paper towels to drain. Discard the water.

2 At least 30 minutes before you are ready to begin grilling, remove the steaks from the refrigerator. When the bacon is cool enough to handle, wrap 2 slices around the edge of each steak, then tie in place with kitchen string, snipping off any excess string. Season the steaks on both sides with salt and pepper. Place the steaks on a platter and brush on both sides with the oil.

3 Prepare a charcoal or gas grill for direct grilling over high heat (page 16 or 18). Brush and oil the grill grate.

4 Place the steaks on the grill directly over the fire, and cook for 4 minutes. Using tongs or a wide spatula, rotate each steak a quarter turn (90 degrees), and continue cooking for 2 minutes, then turn and cook for about another 6 minutes. Two things should be happening: the bacon should be getting crisp, and at the end of 12 minutes, you should have a medium-rare steak. To test, insert an instant-read thermometer horizontally into the center of a steak; it should register 135°F (57°C). If you want to cook the steaks to medium, find a cool spot along the edge of your charcoal grill or cut the burners down on your gas grill to medium heat.

5 Transfer the steaks to warmed plates and let rest for 5–10 minutes. Snip and remove the strings, then spoon the warm sauce over the steaks.

GOES GREAT WITH Grilled Asparagus with Lemon Mayonnaise (page 166); The Best Mashed Potatoes (page 198); Buttery Dinner Rolls (page 207)

Hanger Steak Sliders
with Blue Cheese and Caramelized Onions

4 hanger steaks, each
about 6 oz (185 g)

Balsamic-Mustard Marinade
(page 210)

Canola oil for brushing

1 tablespoon unsalted butter

2 sweet onions, thinly sliced

12 slider rolls, split

¼ lb (125 g) blue cheese,
crumbled

SERVES 6

_____

The Game Plan

- Make marinade; marinate
  steaks overnight

- Remove steaks from fridge
  and discard marinade

- Pat steaks dry and brush
  with oil

- Set up grill for direct grilling
  over high heat

- Slice and cook onions

- Grilling time: 8–12 minutes

- Slice steaks and
  assemble sandwiches

- DON'T FORGET This cut tastes
  best served medium-rare and
  definitely not past medium.

Hanger steak, blue cheese, caramelized onions—how could that combination not be sensational? Once known as the butcher's tenderloin, hanger steak—each animal has only one, located near its diaphragm—has a deep, rich flavor that hold its own alongside tart blue cheese and sweet onions. I've stacked the trio on slider buns just because it's fun.

1 Place the hanger steaks in a large lock-top plastic bag and pour in the marinade. Seal the bag closed, squish the marinade around the meat, and refrigerate overnight.

2 At least 30 minutes before you are ready to begin grilling, remove the steaks from the refrigerator. Discard the marinade and pat the steaks dry with paper towels. Brush the steaks with the oil.

3 Prepare a charcoal or gas grill for direct grilling over high heat (page 16 or 18). Brush and oil the grill grate.

4 In a sauté pan over low heat, melt the butter. Add the onions and cook slowly, stirring often, until they are tender and caramelized, about 20 minutes. Remove from the heat and keep warm. (If necessary, reheat just before serving.)

5 Place the steaks on the grill directly over the fire and cook, turning once, until nicely charred on both sides and barely firm to the touch, about 4 minutes per side for medium-rare or 6 minutes per side for medium.

6 Transfer the steaks to a cutting board and let rest for about 5 minutes. Meanwhile, put the rolls, cut side down, on the edge of the grill to toast for about 1 minute.

7 Thinly slice the steaks against the grain, capturing any released juices. Toss the sliced meat and juices together in a bowl. Divide the meat and juices evenly among the roll bottoms. Top with the cheese and then with the onions, dividing them both evenly. Cap with the roll tops and serve at once.

_____

GOES GREAT WITH Smoky Grilled Potatoes (page 176); Balsamic Onion and Green Bean Salad (page 200); Spinach and Bacon Salad (page 205)

Asian-Style Flank Steak Salad

1 flank steak, about 2 lb (1 kg)

Ginger-Soy Marinade
(page 210)

6 cups (6 oz/185 g) mixed
salad greens

1 bunch radishes, thinly sliced

1 small red onion, thinly sliced

6 tablespoons (2 oz/60 g)
dry-roasted peanuts

¼ cup (2 fl oz/60 ml) canola oil

2 tablespoons rice vinegar

1 teaspoon sweet
hot-pepper sauce

1 tablespoon chopped
fresh chives

Kosher salt and freshly
ground pepper

SERVES 6–8

The Game Plan

- Make marinade; marinate
  steak overnight

- Remove steak from fridge;
  discard marinade; pat dry

- Set up grill for direct grilling
  over high heat

- Grilling time: 8–12 minutes

- Prepare salad greens and
  dressing; slice steak and
  assemble salads

- DON'T FORGET The overnight
  marinade is important—the
  steak is the star here, so you
  want it to be very flavorful.

Flank steak is a protein that really absorbs flavors, so here I've put it into a robust ginger-soy marinade overnight. Of course, you can just grill the steak and forget about the salad, but you will be missing a great combination of tender, flavorful meat; crisp salad greens; crunchy peanuts; and a spicy vinaigrette.

1 Using a sharp knife, make diagonal cuts about 1 inch (2.5 cm) apart and ¼ inch (6 mm) deep across one side of the steak. Place the steak in a large lock-top plastic bag and pour in the marinade. Seal the bag closed, squish the marinade around the steak, and refrigerate overnight.

2 At least 30 minutes before you are ready to begin grilling, remove the steak from the refrigerator. Discard the marinade and pat the steak dry with paper towels.

3 Prepare a charcoal or gas grill for direct grilling over high heat (page 16 or 18). Brush and oil the grill grate.

4 Place the steak on the grill directly over the fire and cook, turning once, until nicely charred on both sides, about 4 minutes on each side for medium-rare or 6 minutes on each side for medium.

5 Transfer the steak to a cutting board and let rest for 10 minutes. Meanwhile, divide the greens among individual bowls or plates. Sprinkle the radish slices, onion slices, and peanuts over the greens, dividing them evenly. In a bowl, whisk together the oil, vinegar, and hot-pepper sauce, then whisk in the chives. Season to taste with salt and pepper.

6 Thinly slice the steak against the grain, capturing any released juices. Arrange the slices on top of the greens, dividing them evenly, and then pour any captured juices over the top. Drizzle the dressing evenly over the salads and serve at once.

GOES GREAT WITH Smoky Grilled Potatoes (page 176); Grilled Pineapple Skewers with Chile-Lime Salt (page 179); Garlic Bread (page 207)

Italian-Style Porterhouse

FOR THE MARINADE

4 cloves garlic, halved

4 fresh oregano sprigs

2 fresh thyme sprigs

¼ cup (2 fl oz/60 ml) extra-virgin olive oil

2 tablespoons red wine vinegar

⅛ teaspoon red pepper flakes

4 porterhouse steaks, each 12–16 oz (375–500 g) and 1½ inches (4 cm) thick

Kosher salt and freshly ground black pepper

Olive oil for brushing

1 tablespoon fresh oregano leaves

1 tablespoon fresh thyme leaves

SERVES 4–8

The Game Plan

- Make marinade; marinate steaks overnight

- Remove steaks from fridge and discard marinade

- Pat steaks dry; season and brush with oil

- Set up grill for direct grilling over high heat

- Grilling time: about 12 minutes

- DON'T FORGET These are big steaks, so depending on who you are feeding, 2 steaks may be plenty for 4 people.

Porterhouse steaks are great for entertaining because each side of the bone gives you a different cut. You get the lean and tender fillet on one side and the bolder-flavored sirloin on the other. Finish the steaks with fresh oregano and thyme, and you will be transported to an alfresco dinner in Tuscany.

1 To make the marinade, in a bowl, mix together the garlic, oregano, thyme, oil, vinegar, and red pepper flakes.

2 Place the steaks in a single layer in a baking dish (or 2 dishes, if necessary), and pour the marinade over the steaks. Turn the steaks to coat both sides, then cover with plastic wrap and refrigerate overnight.

3 At least 30 minutes before you are ready to begin grilling, remove the steaks from the refrigerator. Discard the marinade and pat the steaks dry with paper towels. Season the steaks generously on both sides with salt and pepper.

4 Prepare a charcoal or gas grill for direct grilling over high heat (page 16 or 18). Brush and oil the grill grate.

5 Brush the steaks on both sides with the oil. Place the steaks on the grill directly over the fire and cook for about 3 minutes. Using tongs or a wide spatula, rotate each steak a quarter turn (90 degrees), and continue cooking for another 3 minutes, then turn the steaks. Cook the steaks until well marked and cooked to your liking, about another 6 minutes for medium-rare, or until an instant-read thermometer inserted horizontally into the center of a steak away from bone registers 135°F (57°C).

6 Transfer the steaks to warmed plates and let rest for 5–10 minutes. Sprinkle the steaks evenly with the oregano and thyme. Serve at once.

GOES GREAT WITH Grilled Panzanella Salad (page 188); Grilled Balsamic Onions (page 200); Pesto Pasta Salad (page 201)

Teriyaki Sirloin Steaks

FOR THE TERIYAKI SAUCE

½ cup (4 fl oz/125 ml) pineapple juice

¼ cup (2 fl oz/60 ml) tamari or reduced-sodium soy sauce

¼ cup (2 fl oz/60 ml) Worcestershire sauce

2 tablespoons dry sherry

⅛ teaspoon ground ginger

Garlic salt

4 top sirloin steaks, each 8–10 oz (250–315 g) and about 1½ inches (4 cm) thick

Kosher salt and freshly ground pepper

SERVES 4

The Game Plan

- Make teriyaki sauce; reserve some for serving

- Marinate steaks overnight

- Remove steaks from fridge and discard marinade

- Pat steaks dry and season

- Set up grill for direct grilling over high heat

- Grilling time: about 11 minutes

- Let steaks rest, then slice

- DON'T FORGET Choose top sirloin steaks for the best flavor and texture.

Sirloin steaks are perfect when you have a big dinner with family or friends on the calendar. Fortunately, supermarket meat counters often put them on sale, so watch for a good deal. In this recipe, I have marinated them in my homemade teriyaki sauce, which goes together quickly and beats the bottled brands.

1 To make the teriyaki sauce, in a small saucepan, combine the pineapple juice, tamari, Worcestershire sauce, ¼ cup (2 fl oz/60 ml) water, sherry, ginger, and garlic salt to taste. Place over medium-high heat and bring to a boil. Reduce the heat to medium-low and simmer, stirring occasionally, until slightly thickened, 10–12 minutes. Remove from the heat and let cool completely. You should have about 1 cup (8 fl oz/250 ml). (The sauce can be made up to 1 week in advance and refrigerated. Bring to room temperature before using.)

2 Set aside ¼ cup (2 fl oz/60 ml) of the sauce. Place the steaks in a large lock-top plastic bag and pour in the remaining sauce. Seal the bag closed, squish the sauce around the steaks, and refrigerate overnight.

3 At least 30 minutes before you are ready to begin grilling, remove the steaks from the refrigerator. Discard the sauce and pat the steaks dry with paper towels. Season the steaks on both sides with salt and pepper.

4 Prepare a charcoal or gas grill for direct grilling over high heat (page 16 or 18). Brush and oil the grill grate.

5 Place the steaks on the grill directly over the fire and cook for 3 minutes. Turn and cook for another 3 minutes. Turn again and cook for 5 minutes more for medium-rare, or until an instant-read thermometer inserted horizontally into the center of a steak registers 135°F (57°C).

6 Transfer the steaks to a cutting board and let rest for 5–10 minutes. Slice against the grain, arrange on a platter, and serve at once. Pass the reserved teriyaki sauce at the table.

GOES GREAT WITH Grilled Veggies (page 201); Asian-Style Slaw (page 203); Watermelon Salad (page 203)

Carne Asada Tacos
with Smoky Tomato Salsa

1 skirt steak, about 2 lb (1 kg)

2 tablespoons Latin Spice Rub (page 208)

1 lime, halved, plus lime wedges for serving

4 cloves garlic, coarsely chopped

2 tablespoons chopped fresh cilantro

Kosher salt and freshly ground pepper

Olive oil for brushing

24 corn tortillas, about 6 inches (15 cm) in diameter

Smoky Tomato Salsa (page 214) for serving

2 avocados, pitted, peeled, and sliced

SERVES 6

_____

The Game Plan

- Make spice rub; season steak and refrigerate overnight

- Make salsa; refrigerate

- Remove steak from fridge and brush with oil

- Set up grill for direct grilling over high heat

- Grilling time: 8–12 minutes

- Slice avocados; slice steak; assemble tacos

- DON'T FORGET Slice the steak against the grain to enhance its tenderness: hold the knife at a 45-degree angle and cut into thin slices.

If you live too far from a taco truck to enjoy the real thing as often as you'd like, this recipe solves the problem. It calls for authentic seasonings, the correct cut of meat, and, true to taco-truck tradition, doesn't overstuff the tacos with condiments—just a little smoky salsa and a slice of avocado. If you can find fresh, thick corn tortillas, you'll only need to use one per taco.

1 Sprinkle the steak evenly on both sides with the rub, then squeeze 1 lime half over each side. Rub the garlic and cilantro into both sides of the steak, and then season both sides generously with salt and pepper. Place the steak in a large lock-top plastic bag, seal the bag closed, and refrigerate overnight.

2 At least 30 minutes before you are ready to begin grilling, remove the steak from the refrigerator. Brush the steak on both sides with the oil.

3 Prepare a charcoal or gas grill for direct grilling over high heat (page 16 or 18). Brush and oil the grill grate.

4 Place the steak on the grill directly over the fire and cook, turning once, until nicely charred on both sides and fairly firm to the touch, about 4 minutes per side for medium-rare or 6 minutes per side for medium. (Rare skirt steak can be a little tough. Medium-rare or medium works best.)

5 Transfer the steak to a cutting board and let rest for 5 minutes. Meanwhile, warm the tortillas on the grill, about 1 minute on each side, then stack and wrap in a kitchen towel.

6 Thinly slice the steak against the grain. To assemble each taco, overlap 2 tortillas, top with the meat, add a spoonful of the salsa, and 1 or 2 slices of avocado. Add a lime wedge to each plate. Fold and enjoy.

_____

GOES GREAT WITH Grilled Corn with Lime Butter (page 165); Drunken Pinto Beans (page 194); Mexican Rice (page 197)

Charred Beef Tenderloin
with Chimichurri Sauce

1 whole beef tenderloin,
about 6½ lb (3.26 kg), trimmed

6 cloves garlic, thinly sliced

Kosher salt and freshly
ground pepper

FOR THE CHIMICHURRI SAUCE

½ cup (4 fl oz/125 ml) *each*
extra-virgin olive oil and red
wine vinegar

¼ cup (1½ oz/45 g)
minced red onion

2 tablespoons minced
bell pepper

2 tablespoons minced
fresh flat-leaf parsley

2 teaspoons chopped
fresh oregano

2 teaspoons minced garlic

¼ teaspoon red pepper flakes

Kosher salt and freshly
ground black pepper

SERVES 8–10

The Game Plan

- Stud meat with garlic slices;
  season with salt and pepper

- Make chimichurri; refrigerate

- Set up grill for indirect grilling
  over medium heat

- Grilling time: about 1½ hours

- DON'T FORGET The internal
  temperature of the tenderloin
  will rise 5° to 10°F (3° to 6°C)
  after you pull it from the fire.

A whole beef tenderloin is a luxury cut to serve a crowd. I use direct and indirect heat here, searing the meat well first and then cooking it in gentle reflected heat. I like to top it with my version of Argentina's famous chimichurri sauce, a tangy garlic-herb relish. Serve it with just about any grilled meat or seafood.

1 At least 45 minutes before you are ready to begin grilling, remove the beef tenderloin from the refrigerator. Using a boning or other narrow-bladed knife, cut small, shallow, evenly spaced slits all over the surface of the tenderloin. Slide the garlic slices into the slits. Season the tenderloin generously with salt and pepper.

2 To make the chimichurri sauce, in a bowl, whisk together the oil, vinegar, onion, bell pepper, parsley, oregano, garlic, red pepper flakes, a pinch of salt, and a few grinds of pepper. You should have about 1 cup (8 fl oz/250 ml). Let stand at room temperature for about 30 minutes to allow the flavors to blend. Whisk again just before serving. (The sauce can be made up to 2 days in advance and refrigerated. Bring to room temperature before serving.)

3 Prepare a charcoal or gas grill for indirect grilling over medium heat; the temperature inside the grill should be 350°–375°F (180°–190°C). If using charcoal, bank the lit coals on one side of the grill bed, and place a drip pan in the area without coals (page 16). If using gas, preheat the burners, then turn off 1 or more of the burners to create a cooler zone (page 19). Brush and oil the grill grate.

4 Place the tenderloin on the grill over the direct-heat area. Sear, turning as needed, until nicely browned on all sides, 8–10 minutes total. Move the tenderloin to the indirect-heat area, cover the grill, and cook for 1½ hours for medium-rare, or until an instant-read thermometer inserted in the thickest part of the meat registers 135°F (57°C).

5 Transfer to a cutting board and let rest for 15 minutes. Thinly slice the tenderloin against the grain and arrange on a platter. Spoon the chimichurri sauce over the beef. Serve warm or at room temperature.

GOES GREAT WITH Grilled Romaine Salad (page 170); Grilled Veggies (page 201); Buttery Dinner Rolls (page 207)

Korean Short Ribs

FOR THE MARINADE

½ cup (4 fl oz/125 ml) reduced-sodium soy sauce

¼ cup (2 oz/60 g) firmly packed light brown sugar

2 tablespoons rice vinegar

2 tablespoons Asian sesame oil

2 tablespoons minced garlic

1 tablespoon peeled and finely chopped fresh ginger

1 tablespoon ketchup

1 teaspoon red pepper flakes

5 lb (2.5 kg) flanken-cut beef short ribs, prepared by your butcher

1 cup (8 fl oz/250 ml) Asian-Style BBQ Sauce (page 212)

SERVES 6

The Game Plan

- Make marinade; marinate ribs overnight

- Make Asian-style BBQ sauce; refrigerate

- Remove ribs from fridge and discard marinade; pat dry

- Set up grill for direct grilling over high heat

- Grilling time: 6–8 minutes

- Brush with BBQ sauce during last 2 minutes

- DON'T FORGET Unlike thicker ribs that are cooked slowly over low heat, these thin ribs want a quick sear, and should be cooked no further than medium.

This restaurant classic is infused with plenty of sweet, salty, hot, and tangy flavors. You need to marinate the ribs overnight, but after that, nothing takes much time: the ribs spend hardly any time on the grill, and then after a short rest, everybody can eat. The marinade and sauce are great on chicken or pork, too.

1 To make the marinade, in a large bowl, combine the soy sauce, sugar, vinegar, sesame oil, garlic, ginger, ketchup, and red pepper flakes and whisk to dissolve the sugar. Place the ribs in a large lock-top plastic bag and pour in the marinade. Seal the bag closed, squish the marinade around the ribs, and refrigerate the bag overnight. Be sure to turn the bag over several times while the ribs are marinating.

2 Prepare a charcoal or gas grill for direct grilling over high heat (page 16 or 18). Brush and oil the grill grate.

3 Remove the ribs from the marinade and discard the marinade. Pat the ribs dry with paper towels.

4 Place the ribs on the grill directly over the fire and cook, turning once, until medium, 6–8 minutes total. During the last 2 minutes of cooking, brush the ribs with some of the BBQ sauce.

5 Transfer the ribs to a platter and let rest for 5–10 minutes. Serve at once with the remaining BBQ sauce on the side.

GOES GREAT WITH Coconut Rice (page 196); Asian-Style Slaw (page 203); Cucumber Salad (page 203)

How to smoke the perfect
Brisket

More cooks have trouble turning out a good smoked beef brisket than almost anything else from the grill. Of course, folks in Texas seem to have no trouble, but that's because most of them have been smoking brisket since they were able to walk. Fortunately, the secret to success comes to just five basic rules.

BUY THE RIGHT SIZE Thin cuts of brisket cook very fast, so they don't have time to absorb the smoky flavor. Buy a brisket that is about 3 inches (7.5 cm) thick and has a fair amount of fat. Since smoking a brisket is going to take a while, you might as well cook a whole brisket. The leftovers, if you have any, freeze well.

DON'T OVERSEASON Lots of television cooking shows and books will push you to season the brisket with all kinds of things. But the guys in Texas who taught me how to smoke a brisket rarely use anything other than salt, pepper, and granulated garlic. They let the wood and smoke do the seasoning.

CHOOSE THE RIGHT WOOD Mesquite is traditional. It burns hotter than other common woods, like hickory or oak.

GO LOW AND SLOW A good smoked brisket—meltingly tender, full flavored—is all about patience. You need to maintain a steady, low temperature of 200°–250°F (95°–120°C) in a covered grill or smoker and you need time—at least 6 hours—but it's worth every minute. (If you run out of time or wood, finish the brisket in the oven. You are the only one who will know you did it.)

WRAP IT UP If you are not going to be eating the brisket right away, wrap it up in aluminum foil for a few hours to prevent it from drying out.

GOES GREAT WITH A side of beans is a given. Try the Smoky Baked Beans with Bacon (page 194) or even the Southwestern Bean Salad (page 195). And don't forget some slaw: I like my brisket with Creamy Coleslaw (page 202).

Texas-Style BBQ Brisket

1 beef brisket, about 5 lb (2.5 kg),
fat trimmed to ½ inch (12 mm)

Kosher salt and freshly
ground pepper

1 tablespoon granulated garlic

About 8 cups wood chips,
preferably mesquite, soaked
in water for 30 minutes

Perfect Brisket BBQ Sauce
(page 212) for serving

---

1 At least 1 hour before you are ready to begin cooking, remove the brisket from the refrigerator. Season the brisket generously all over with salt and pepper. Sprinkle the garlic evenly over the brisket, then gently rub it into the surface.

2 Prepare a smoker (page 8) or a charcoal or gas grill for smoking over low heat (page 17 or 19). You want to smoke this brisket very low and very slow, so the temperature of the grill should be 200°–250°F (95°–120°C). If using charcoal, bank the lit coals on either side of the grill bed, leaving a strip in the center without heat. Place a drip pan in the center strip and fill the pan with water. Add about 2 cups of the wood chips to the fire just before grilling. If using gas, fill the smoker box with up to 2 cups of the wood chips, then preheat the grill. Turn off 1 or more of the burners to create a cooler zone. Brush and oil the grill grate.

3 Place the brisket on the grill over the indirect-heat area and cover the grill. Smoke the meat for about 2 hours, adding additional wood chips every 30 minutes or so and more coals as needed if using charcoal.

4 Remove the brisket from the grill and wrap it in aluminum foil. You can put it back in the smoker or on the grill and cook it slowly for another 4 hours (I don't recommend this if you are using charcoal), or you can place it in a roasting pan in a 250°F (120°C) oven for an additional 4 hours. The brisket is ready when it is fork-tender.

5 Transfer the brisket to a cutting board and remove the foil. Let rest for 10–15 minutes. Thinly slice against the grain, arrange the slices on a platter, and serve at once. Serve the BBQ sauce—reheated or at room temperature—on the side.

SERVES 10–12

Chile-Rubbed Smoked Tri-Tip

1 tri-tip roast, 3 lb (1.5 kg)

1 tablespoon chile powder

1 teaspoon garlic salt

Freshly ground pepper

About 4 cups wood chips, soaked in water, beer, or apple cider for 30 minutes

Pico de Gallo (page 215) for serving

SERVES 6–8
WITH LEFTOVERS

The Game Plan

- Make pico de gallo; refrigerate
- Remove tri-tip from fridge; rub with spices
- Soak wood chips; set up grill for smoking over medium heat
- Grilling time: 1–1½ hours
- Let meat rest, then slice
- DON'T FORGET An instant-read thermometer is your best guide for doneness; be sure to insert it into the thickest part of the roast.

This dish is to central California what pulled pork is to North Carolina. The first time I had tri-tip this way was at a convenience store in the heart of artichoke country, south of San Francisco. It was cooked on a gas grill out behind the store, and it was so good, I talked the cook out of his recipe. Here it is.

1 At least 1 hour before you are ready to begin cooking, remove the roast from the refrigerator. Season the roast on all sides with the chile powder, garlic salt, and a generous amount of pepper.

2 Prepare a charcoal or gas grill for smoking over medium heat (page 17 or 19); the temperature inside the grill should be 350°–375°F (180°–190°C). If using charcoal, bank the lit coals on either side of the grill bed, leaving a strip in the center without heat. Place a drip pan in the center strip and fill the pan with water. Add about 2 cups of the wood chips to the fire just before grilling. If using gas, fill the smoker box with up to 2 cups of the wood chips, then preheat the grill. Turn off 1 or more of the burners to create a cooler zone. Brush and oil the grill grate.

3 Place the roast on the grill over the direct-heat area and sear, turning as needed, until browned but not charred on all sides, about 15–20 minutes total. Move the roast to the indirect-heat area, cover the grill, and cook for about 45 minutes for medium-rare or 1 hour for medium, adding the remaining wood chips after about 30 minutes. Tri-tip roasts come in different shapes—some are squat, and some are more rounded—so cooking times will vary. Remove the roast when an instant-read thermometer inserted into the thickest part registers 135°F (57°C) for medium-rare or 140°F (60°C) for medium.

4 Transfer the roast to a cutting board, tent with aluminum foil, and let rest for 15 minutes. Slice very thinly against the grain, capturing any released juices, and arrange on a platter. Pour any accumulated juices over the top and serve at once with the pico de gallo.

GOES GREAT WITH Drunken Pinto Beans (page 194); Creamy Coleslaw (page 202); Skillet Corn Bread (page 206)

Smoky Beef Ribs

2 racks beef ribs, 8 bones each

2 teaspoons granulated garlic

Kosher salt and freshly
ground pepper

About 4 cups wood chips,
soaked in water for 30 minutes

Perfect Brisket BBQ Sauce
(page 212), or your favorite
BBQ sauce, for serving

SERVES 4

The Game Plan

- Make BBQ sauce; refrigerate

- Remove racks from fridge
  and season

- Soak wood chips; set up
  smoker or grill for smoking
  over low heat

- Grilling time: about 2 hours

- Let racks rest, then slice

- DON'T FORGET When you're
  shopping for beef ribs, look
  for ribs with plenty of meat
  and not too much fat.

Beef ribs are seldom cooked on a grill, and that's too bad. Yes, if you cook them too fast and at too hot a temperature, they turn out burnt, tough, and hard to eat. But if you use a smoker or indirect heat to cook them low and slow, you'll end up with a pile of juicy ribs bursting with flavor.

1 At least 1 hour before you are ready to begin grilling, remove the ribs from the refrigerator. Remove the thin membrane from the back of each rack (page 94) and trim off excess fat. Season the ribs on both sides with the garlic and with generous amounts of salt and pepper.

2 Prepare a smoker (page 8) or a charcoal or gas grill for smoking over low heat (page 17 or 19); the temperature inside the grill should be 200°–250°F (95°–120°C). If using charcoal, bank the lit coals on either side of the grill bed, leaving a strip in the center without heat. Place a drip pan in the center strip and fill the pan with water. Add about 1 cup of the wood chips to the fire just before grilling. If using gas, fill the smoker box with about 1 cup of the wood chips, then preheat the grill. Turn off 1 or more of the burners to create a cooler zone. Brush and oil the grill grate.

3 Place the ribs, bone side down, on the grill over the indirect-heat area. Cover the grill and cook until tender, about 2 hours, adding additional wood chips every 30 minutes or so and more coals as needed if using charcoal.

4 Transfer the racks to a cutting board and let rest for 10 minutes. Slice off a rib and give it a taste. It should be tender but should still take some bite to pull it from the bone. Cut the racks into individual ribs and pile on a platter. Serve at once with the BBQ sauce.

GOES GREAT WITH Potato Salad (page 195); Lexington-Style Slaw (page 202); Garlic Bread (page 207)

Smoked Prime Rib
with Fresh Horseradish Sauce

1 bone-in standing rib roast,
5–6 lb (2.5–3 kg), trimmed
of excess fat

6 large cloves garlic

¼ cup (¼ oz/7 g) lightly
packed fresh rosemary leaves

¼ cup (¼ oz/7 g) lightly
packed fresh basil leaves

Kosher salt and freshly
ground pepper

3 tablespoons Dijon mustard

3 tablespoons olive oil

About 4 cups wood chips,
soaked in water for 30 minutes

Fresh Horseradish Sauce
(page 216) for serving

SERVES 8–10

The Game Plan

- Make horseradish sauce;
  refrigerate

- Remove roast from fridge;
  make seasoning paste and
  spread on roast

- Soak wood chips; set up
  smoker or grill for smoking
  over medium heat

- Grilling time: 1½–2 hours

- Let meat rest, then slice

- DON'T FORGET This is a huge
  roast, so you really want to
  let it sit for at least 20 minutes
  before you carve it.

In the 1980s, prime rib had become so ubiquitous on restaurant menus that it fell out of favor with many diners. Fortunately, savvy cooks know better. Taking the time to smoke a prime rib adds even more flavor to an already flavorful cut. Don't skip the horseradish sauce: its tart, slightly acidic character heightens the smoke flavor of the beef.

1 At least 1 hour before you are ready to begin cooking, remove the roast from the refrigerator. In a food processor, combine the garlic, rosemary, basil, and 2 teaspoons each salt and pepper. Pulse to mince finely. Add the mustard and pulse to combine. With the motor running, slowly pour in the oil and process until a paste forms. Smear the paste evenly over the entire surface of the roast.

2 Prepare a smoker (page 8) or a charcoal or gas grill for smoking over medium heat (page 17 or 19); the temperature inside the grill should be 350°–375°F (180°–190°C). If using charcoal, bank the lit coals on either side of the grill bed, leaving a strip in the center without heat. Place a drip pan in the center strip and fill the pan with water. Add about 1 cup of the wood chips to the fire just before grilling. If using gas, fill the smoker box with about 1 cup of the wood chips, then preheat the grill. Turn off 1 or more of the burners to create a cooler zone. Brush and oil the grill grate.

3 Place the roast, bone side down, on the grill over the indirect-heat area. Cover the grill and cook to your liking, 1½–2 hours for medium-rare, adding additional wood chips every 30 minutes or so and more coals as needed if using charcoal. The roast is ready when an instant-read thermometer inserted into the center of the meat away from bone registers 130°–135°F (54°–57°C).

4 Transfer the roast to a cutting board, tent with aluminum foil, and let rest for 20–30 minutes. Using a sharp knife, remove the bones from the roast. Carve the meat into thin slices and arrange on a warmed platter. Serve at once with the horseradish sauce.

GOES GREAT WITH Creamed Spinach (page 198); Cheesy Cauliflower Gratin (page 199); Iceberg Wedge with Blue Cheese (page 204)

How to grill the perfect
Lamb Chops

I treat lamb loin chops much like I do T-bone steaks: I'm shooting for a good char on the outside and a juicy, pink center. That plan makes good sense because a lamb loin chop has its own T-bone. Here are four simple rules for successfully grilling lamb chops.

GO FOR BOLD FLAVORS Lamb is made to carry the flavors of rosemary and garlic. They complement the light gaminess and deep richness of the meat. But you can switch out the rosemary for mint or thyme, and you can punch up the flavor with a squeeze of lemon juice.

BUY QUALITY Good-quality lamb chops are bursting with flavor. Locally raised grass-fed lamb is a great choice for its big flavor. If you can't find local lamb, look for meat from Down Under. New Zealand and Australia are both known for their mild, tender, delicious lamb.

CHOOSE THE RIGHT CUT You want to grill the chops medium-rare, and that's easier to achieve if you buy chops that are at least 1 inch (2.5 cm) thick or opt for double-cut rib chops. Thick T-bone loin chops are the best choice, however, because you get some tenderloin and some of the more flavorful sirloin.

DON'T OVERCOOK It's sad but true: most people overcook lamb. To avoid that mistake, use the same touch method you used for steak. Remember? Medium-rare feels like the tip of your nose. When chops feel like that, get them off the grill right away and let them rest for a few minutes before serving.

GOES GREAT WITH I like to serve lamb chops with grilled vegetables (page 201), especially zucchini when it's at full tilt in the summertime. You can throw the veggies right on the grill with the chops.

Rosemary-Garlic Lamb Chops

2 tablespoons finely chopped
fresh rosemary

4 cloves garlic, finely chopped

Kosher salt and freshly ground pepper

8 lamb T-bone loin chops, about 1 inch
(2.5 cm) thick

2 tablespoons olive oil

---

1 On a cutting board, using a chef's or other large knife, work together the rosemary, garlic, a big pinch of salt, and several grinds of pepper into a paste. Rub the mixture evenly over both sides of the lamb chops, then brush both sides with the oil. Place on a platter, cover with plastic wrap, and refrigerate for 30 minutes.

2 At least 30 minutes before you are ready to begin grilling, remove the chops from the refrigerator.

3 Prepare a charcoal or gas grill for direct grilling over high heat (page 16 or 18). Brush and oil the grill grate.

4 Place the chops on the grill and cook, turning once, until nicely charred and done to your liking, about 4 minutes on each side for medium-rare—perfect for lamb chops.

5 Transfer to a platter and let rest for about 5 minutes. Serve at once.

SERVES 4

Lamb Chops
with Mediterranean Tapenade

FOR THE MARINADE

½ cup (4 fl oz/125 ml) extra-virgin olive oil

2 tablespoons whole-grain mustard

2 cloves garlic, crushed and finely minced

1 tablespoon dry vermouth

1 tablespoon fresh oregano

4 or 5 juniper berries, crushed with the back of a knife

2 lamb racks, each with 8 chops and about 2 lb (1 kg), frenched

Mediterranean Tapenade (page 214) for serving

SERVES 6–8

The Game Plan

- Make marinade; marinate racks overnight
- Make tapenade; refrigerate
- Remove racks from fridge; discard marinade; pat dry
- Set up grill for indirect grilling over medium heat
- Grilling time: 18–25 minutes
- Let racks rest, then slice
- DON'T FORGET Be careful not to overcook these—you can always throw the chops back on the grill for a quick sear if they are too rare.

Lamb chops are naturally tasty, so they don't need a lot of dressing up. But this quick marinade, which echoes the flavors of a martini, delivers an interesting edge to the rich lamb. The tapenade recipe adds sun-dried tomatoes to the usual olives for a sunny accompaniment that is also a delicious topping for grilled fish and chicken.

1 To make the marinade, in a small bowl, whisk together the oil, mustard, garlic, vermouth, oregano, and juniper berries. Place the lamb racks in a large lock-top plastic bag. Pour the marinade into the bag, seal the bag closed, squish the marinade around the meat, and refrigerate overnight.

2 At least 30 minutes before you are ready to begin grilling, remove the racks from the refrigerator. Discard the marinade and lightly pat the racks dry with paper towels. You want to leave a little of the marinade clinging to the meat.

3 Prepare a charcoal or gas grill for indirect grilling over medium heat; the temperature inside the grill should be 350°–375°F (180°–190°C). If using charcoal, bank the lit coals on either side of the grill bed, leaving a strip in the center without heat, and place a drip pan in the center strip (page 16). If using gas, preheat the burners, then turn off 1 or more of the burners to create a cooler zone (page 19). Brush and oil the grill grate.

4 Place the racks on the grill over the direct-heat area and sear, turning as needed, until nicely browned on all sides, 3–5 minutes total. Move the racks to the indirect-heat area and cook until done to your liking, 15–20 minutes for medium-rare, or until the thickest part of each rack yields easily to the touch, or an instant-read thermometer inserted in the thickest part away from bone registers 135°F (57°C).

5 Transfer to a cutting board and let rest for about 5 minutes. Cut the racks into individual chops and serve with the tapenade.

GOES GREAT WITH The Best Mashed Potatoes (page 198); Grilled Veggies (page 201); Garlic Bread (page 207)

Moroccan Leg of Lamb
with Tangy Pomegranate Glaze

FOR THE POMEGRANATE GLAZE

1 cup (11 oz/345 g) pomegranate molasses

¼ cup (2 oz/60 g) well-drained prepared horseradish

1 tablespoon Dijon mustard

Kosher salt and coarsely ground pepper

1 boneless leg of lamb, 3 lb (1.5 kg), butterflied

North African Spice Rub (page 209)

¼ cup (¼ oz/7 g) chopped fresh mint leaves

SERVES 6

The Game Plan

- Make glaze; refrigerate

- Remove lamb from fridge; make spice rub; season lamb with rub

- Set up grill for indirect grilling over high heat

- Grilling time: about 1 hour

- Brush lamb with glaze during last 5 minutes

- Brush again with glaze, let rest, then slice

- DON'T FORGET Ask your butcher to butterfly the leg of lamb for you.

Cooks living around the Mediterranean are old hands at grilled lamb. This recipe, which marries a butterflied leg of lamb with a North African–inspired spice rub and a tart pomegranate glaze, is a nod to that tradition. Save yourself some time and ask the butcher to bone and butterfly the leg for you. Be sure to tote the bone home to make stock.

1 To make the glaze, in a small bowl, whisk together the pomegranate molasses, horseradish, mustard, and ½ teaspoon each salt and pepper. (The glaze can be made up to 2 days in advance and refrigerated. Bring to room temperature before using.)

2 At least 30 minutes before you are ready to begin grilling, remove the lamb from the refrigerator. Season the lamb on all sides with the spice rub.

3 Prepare a charcoal or gas grill for indirect grilling over high heat; the temperature inside the grill should be 400°–450°F (200°–230°C). If using charcoal, bank the lit coals on one side of the grill bed, and place a drip pan in the area without coals (page 16). If using gas, preheat the burners, then turn off 1 or more of the burners to create a cooler zone (page 19). Brush and oil the grill grate.

4 Place the lamb on the grill over the direct-heat area, cover the grill, and cook for about 10 minutes. Lamb is fatty, so the fire may flare up. Move the lamb to the indirect-heat area, re-cover the grill, and cook for another 10 minutes. Continue cooking and turning about every 5 minutes until done to your liking, about 45 minutes total for medium-rare, or until an instant-read thermometer inserted into the thickest part of the leg registers 135°F (57°C). About 5 minutes before the lamb is done, brush it with the glaze.

5 Transfer the lamb to a cutting board, brush once again with the glaze, tent with aluminum foil, and let rest for 10 minutes. The lamb will be nice and crusty, but because butterflied lamb always has different thicknesses, it will be medium-rare in some spots and medium in others, which should suit everyone at your dinner table. Slice against the grain and arrange on a warmed platter. Sprinkle with the mint and serve at once.

GOES GREAT WITH Grilled Asparagus with Lemon Mayonnaise (page 166); Herbed Rice Pilaf (page 197); Buttery Dinner Rolls (page 207)

Lamb and Vegetable Kebabs
with Indian Spices

2 lb (1 kg) boneless leg of lamb, trimmed of excess fat and cut into 1-inch (2.5-cm) chunks

2 tablespoons garam masala spice blend

6–12 metal or wooden skewers

2 green bell peppers, seeded and cut into slices 1 inch (2.5 cm) thick

2 Asian eggplants, cut crosswise into slices 1 inch (2.5 cm) thick

6 green onions, trimmed to about 3 inches (7.5 cm) of white and pale green

6 cherry tomatoes

SERVES 6

The Game Plan

- Cut lamb into chunks; season and refrigerate for 6 hours or up to overnight

- Remove lamb from fridge; soak skewers if using wooden

- Prepare vegetables

- Set up grill for direct grilling over high heat

- Skewer lamb and vegetables

- Grilling time: 12–15 minutes

- DON'T FORGET Cut the lamb into same-sized chunks so the meat will cook evenly.

These intensely flavored kebabs are seasoned with garam masala, a typical dry spice blend of India that you can find in most well-stocked grocery stores and specialty markets. The blend, which usually includes nutmeg, cumin, cinnamon, cardamom, and fennel, has a hint of sweetness that pairs well with the natural gaminess of lamb.

1 Season the lamb chunks on all sides with the garam masala. Cover and refrigerate for at least 6 hours or up to overnight.

2 At least 1 hour before you are ready to begin grilling, remove the lamb from the refrigerator. If using wooden skewers, soak in water for at least 30 minutes.

3 Prepare a charcoal or gas grill for direct grilling over high heat (page 16 or 18). Brush and oil the grill grate.

4 Thread the lamb chunks, bell pepper and eggplant pieces, green onions, and cherry tomatoes onto the skewers, dividing them evenly. Make sure each skewer starts with a chunk of lamb and ends with a chunk of lamb.

5 Place the skewers on the grill directly over the fire and cook, turning frequently, until nicely browned, 12–15 minutes total. You want the lamb to be medium-rare to medium, so it should feel like the tip of your nose when gently pressed.

6 Transfer the skewers to a platter and let rest for 5 minutes. Slide the lamb and the vegetables off the skewers onto the platter and serve at once.

GOES GREAT WITH Smoky Grilled Potatoes (page 176); Herbed Rice Pilaf (page 197); Grilled Veggies (page 201)

How to grill the perfect
Pork Tenderloin

Pork tenderloins are perfect for the grill
and for our hectic lifestyles because they
cook fairly quickly and can feed a lot of
folks. Here are a couple of tricks to make
the most succulent grilled pork tenderloin.

REMOVE THE SILVER SKIN Nobody wants to eat
that tough stuff, but more importantly, it affects
the cooking time. Some folks like to fold in the
thinner tail part of the tenderloin and tie it with
butcher's twine, which is not a bad idea. That way
you have even thickness throughout the tenderloin.

DON'T OVERCOOK All the nasty bugs you hear
about from undercooked pork are deceased by
the time the pork reaches an internal temperature
of 140°F (60°C). I like to pull pork tenderloins at
about 145°F (63°C), let them rest for 5 to 10 minutes,
and let the residual heat increase the temperature
to about 150°F (65°C). This produces a fantastically
juicy pork tenderloin cooked to medium, which
will be a bit pink in the center. It will break you of
any overcooking habits.

NOT TOO HOT I also think that pork tenderloins need
to be cooked over medium heat. Too high of a heat
causes the proteins to get in an uproar and toughens
the meat, no matter how long it cooks on the grill.

GOES GREAT WITH Slice the tenderloin crosswise
and serve the medallions over just about anything,
from a bed of Vinegar-Braised Collard Greens
(page 199) or Herbed Rice Pilaf (page 197) to a big
helping of creamy mashed potatoes (page 198) or
even decadent Mac and Cheese (page 196).

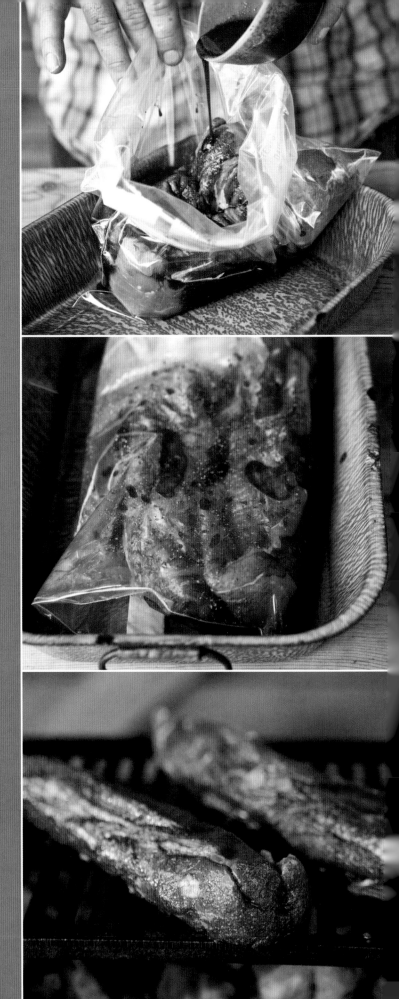

Mustard-Glazed Pork Tenderloin

FOR THE MARINADE

½ cup (4 fl oz/125 ml) tamari or reduced-sodium soy sauce

¼ cup (2 oz/60 g) firmly packed light brown sugar

2 tablespoons dry sherry

½ teaspoon granulated garlic

½ teaspoon ground cinnamon

2 pork tenderloins, each 1½–2 lb (750 g–1 kg), silver skin removed

1 jar (10 oz/315 g) red currant jelly

2 tablespoons Dijon, English, or other spicy mustard

---

1 To make the marinade, in a small bowl, stir together the tamari, sugar, sherry, garlic, and cinnamon. Place the pork in a large lock-top plastic bag and pour in the marinade. Seal the bag closed, squish the marinade around the pork, and refrigerate for at least 4 hours, or overnight is better.

2 At least 30 minutes before you plan to begin grilling, remove the pork from the refrigerator. Discard the marinade and pat the tenderloins dry with paper towels.

3 To make the glaze, in a saucepan over low heat, combine the jelly and mustard and heat until the jelly melts. Do not stir until just before the jelly has melted. Set aside at room temperature.

4 Prepare a charcoal or gas grill for direct grilling over medium heat (page 16 or 18). Brush and oil the grill grate.

5 Place the tenderloins on the grill directly over the fire and cook until nicely grill-marked, 3–4 minutes. Roll them about one-quarter turn, brush the cooked side with the glaze, and cook for another 3–4 minutes. Roll and brush again, then continue in this manner for a total of about 15 minutes for medium. If the glaze begins to burn, move the tenderloins to the edge of the charcoal grill or lower the heat of the gas grill. The pork is ready when it feels fairly firm to the touch, or an instant-read thermometer inserted into the thickest part registers 145°F (63°C). The internal temperature of the tenderloins will rise a few degrees as they rest.

6 Transfer the tenderloins to a cutting board, brush one more time with the glaze, and let rest for about 5 minutes. Slice on the diagonal against the grain and arrange the slices on a platter. Brush with any remaining glaze and serve at once.

SERVES 4–6

Orange Mojo Pork Tenderloin

FOR THE ORANGE MOJO

2 tablespoons cumin seeds

1½ cups (12 fl oz/375 ml) extra-virgin olive oil

4 jalapeño chiles, seeded and finely chopped

12 cloves garlic, minced

Salt and freshly ground pepper

¾ cup (6 fl oz/180 ml) fresh orange juice

¼ cup (⅓ oz/10 g) chopped fresh cilantro

¼ cup (⅓ oz/10 g) chopped fresh oregano

3 tablespoons sherry

2 pork tenderloins, each 1½–2 lb (750 g–1 kg), silver skin removed

2 tablespoons Latin Spice Rub (page 208)

SERVES 4–6

The Game Plan

- Make mojo and spice rub

- Season pork; marinate for 4 hours or up to overnight

- Set up grill for direct grilling over medium heat

- Grilling time: about 15 minutes

- Let pork rest, then slice

- DON'T FORGET Roll the tenderloins a quarter turn every few minutes so that they cook evenly.

Here is a recipe that is easy enough for a midweek dinner (if you marinate the pork the night before) and showy enough for company. A brightly flavored Latin spice rub and a marinade of orange juice, fresh herbs, a dozen garlic cloves, and some jalapeños delivers enough flavor to satisfy the fussiest palates.

1 To make the mojo, in a frying pan over medium heat, toast the cumin seeds, shaking the pan often, until aromatic, about 30 seconds. Add the oil and heat until warm. Add the chiles, garlic, and 1 teaspoon each salt and pepper and heat for 3–5 minutes to blend the flavors. Remove from the heat. In a blender, combine the orange juice, cilantro, oregano, and sherry. Pour in the warm oil mixture and blend until smooth. You should have about 2¾ cups (22 fl oz/680 ml). Divide the mixture in half and let cool. (The mojo can be made in advance and refrigerated for up to 2 days. Bring to room temperature before using.)

2 Rub the pork tenderloins evenly with the Latin spice rub. Place the pork tenderloins in a large lock-top plastic bag and pour in half of the mojo. Seal the bag closed, squish the marinade around the tenderloins, and refrigerate for at least 4 hours, or overnight is better.

3 At least 30 minutes before you plan to begin grilling, remove the pork from the refrigerator. Discard the marinade and lightly pat the tenderloins dry with paper towels.

4 Prepare a charcoal or gas grill for direct grilling over medium heat (page 16 or 18). Brush and oil the grill grate.

5 Place the tenderloins on the grill directly over the fire and cook until nicely grill-marked, 3–4 minutes. Roll them about one-quarter turn and cook for another 3–4 minutes. Continue to roll and cook in this manner for a total of about 15 minutes for medium. The pork is ready when it feels fairly firm to the touch, or an instant-read thermometer inserted into the thickest part registers 145°F (63°C). The internal temperature of the tenderloins will rise a few degrees as they rest.

6 Transfer the tenderloins to a cutting board and let rest for about 5 minutes. Slice on the diagonal against the grain and arrange the slices on a platter. Serve at once with the remaining mojo.

GOES GREAT WITH Southwestern Bean Salad (page 195); Grilled Veggies (page 201); Garlic Bread (page 207)

Brat Sandwiches
with Grilled Peppers and Onions

6 cans (12 fl oz/375 ml each)
lager-style beer

8 fresh bratwurst (about 2 lb/1 kg)

2 large yellow onions,
coarsely chopped

3 green bell peppers, halved
lengthwise and seeded

3 red onions, thickly sliced
into rings

Canola oil for drizzling

8 hoagie rolls, split

Whole-grain mustard
for spreading

Sauerkraut for serving (optional)

SERVES 8

___

The Game Plan

- Simmer brats in beer mixture for 30 minutes

- Set up grill for indirect grilling over medium heat

- Prepare peppers and onions

- Grilling time: about 15 minutes

- Chop peppers and onions; assemble rolls

- DON'T FORGET The beer bath helps keep the brats moist, but don't let them sit on the grill too long or they will dry out.

When the kids are screaming for hot dogs and you want something bolder, throw some beer-braised brats on the grill. They make great football food, at the stadium or in front of the TV. Keep one caveat in mind, however: no ketchup is allowed or you may have folks from Wisconsin hunting you down.

1 In a large pot over high heat, combine the beer, sausages, and yellow onions and bring to a boil. Reduce the heat to medium and simmer gently for about 30 minutes. The brats can sit in this mixture, off the heat, for up to 2 hours. (In case you get distracted.)

2 Prepare a charcoal or gas grill for indirect grilling over medium heat; the temperature inside the grill should be 350°–375°F (180°–190°C). If using charcoal, bank the lit coals on either side (or on one side) of the grill bed, and place a drip pan in the area without coals (page 16). If using gas, preheat the burners, then turn off 1 or more of the burners to create a cooler zone (page 19). Brush and oil the grill grate.

3 Remove the brats from their beer bath, and discard the bath. Drizzle the peppers and red onions with a little oil.

4 Place the brats, bell peppers, and red onions on the grill over the direct-heat area and sear, turning occasionally, until nicely grill-marked, about 2 minutes. Move the brats, peppers, and onions to the indirect-heat area and cook, turning frequently, but letting everything get a nice char, about 15 minutes. The vegetables should be tender but not wilted. During the last minute of cooking, place the rolls, cut side down, along the edge of the grill and grill for 1 or 2 minutes until toasted.

5 Transfer the brats to a large platter and set the rolls to one side. On a cutting board, coarsely chop the red onions and peppers. Spread the cut sides of the rolls with the mustard. Place a brat in each roll and cover with the onion-pepper mixture. Spoon some sauerkraut on top, if desired. Pop a cold one and enjoy.

___

GOES GREAT WITH Smoky Baked Beans with Bacon (page 194); Potato Salad (page 195); Chopped Salad (page 204)

Andouille Sausages
with Sauerkraut and Beer Mustard

FOR THE BEER MUSTARD

1 tablespoon dry mustard

2 tablespoons lager-style beer

¼ cup (2 oz/60 g) prepared Cajun-style mustard

1 tablespoon finely chopped shallot

1 tablespoon firmly packed light brown sugar

1 teaspoon balsamic vinegar

Kosher salt

6 andouille sausages, about 2 lb (1 kg) total weight

1 jar (1 lb/500 g) prepared sauerkraut, drained then heated if desired

SERVES 4

The Game Plan

- Make beer mustard

- Set up grill for direct grilling over high heat

- Grilling time: 10–15 minutes

- Let sausages rest, then slice

- DON'T FORGET Use tongs to turn the sausages often so they cook evenly and don't burn on one side.

Looking for a change from the usual grilled hot dogs or bratwurst? Try Cajun andouille, a highly seasoned smoked pork sausage. Andouille sausages are easy to grill—they just need to be heated through—and taste wonderful alongside sauerkraut, homemade beer mustard, and a pile of smoky potatoes.

1 To make the beer mustard, in a bowl, whisk the dry mustard into the beer to form a paste. Whisk in the prepared mustard, shallot, brown sugar, and vinegar. Season with salt. (The mustard can be made up to 2 weeks in advance and refrigerated.)

2 Prepare a charcoal or gas grill for direct grilling over high heat (page 16 or 18). Brush and oil the grill grate.

3 Place the sausages on the grill directly over the fire and cook, turning often, until browned and heated through, 10–15 minutes.

4 Transfer the sausages to a cutting board and let rest for about 5 minutes. Cut on the diagonal into thick slices. Line a platter with the sauerkraut and top with the sausage slices. Pass the mustard at the table.

GOES GREAT WITH Grilled Baby Artichokes with Spicy Garlic Butter (page 175); Smoky Grilled Potatoes (page 176); Balsamic Onion and Green Bean Salad (page 200)

Spicy Pork Kebabs

FOR THE CILANTRO MARINADE

1 can (14 fl oz/430 ml)
coconut milk

1 bunch fresh cilantro

2 cloves garlic, crushed

1 chipotle chile in adobo sauce

1 tablespoon ground coriander

Kosher salt and freshly
ground pepper

1 lime wedge

2 pork tenderloins, each 1½ lb
(1.5 kg), silver skin removed and
cut into 1-inch (2.5-cm) cubes

6–12 metal or wooden skewers

2 sweet potatoes, peeled and
cut into 1-inch (2.5-cm) cubes

SERVES 4–6

The Game Plan

- Make marinade; cube
  pork; marinate for 4 hours
  or up to overnight

- Remove pork from fridge
  and discard marinade; soak
  skewers if using wooden

- Cube sweet potatoes; boil
  for 5 minutes

- Set up grill for direct grilling
  over high heat

- Skewer pork and potatoes

- Grilling time: about
  10 minutes

- DON'T FORGET Boil the sweet
  potatoes so they are done at
  the same time as the pork.

Pork tenderloins are grill friendly because they cook quickly and stay tender. Plus, they are like sponges: they soak up all the flavors you put around them. This combination of pork tenderloin, cilantro marinade, and sweet potatoes has a Caribbean vibe. Include this dish on the menu the next time you're planning a tailgate party.

1 To make the marinade, in a blender or food processor, combine the coconut milk, cilantro, garlic, chile, and coriander. Pulse to combine, and then process until the mixture is smooth. Add 1 teaspoon pepper and a squeeze of lime juice and process to mix. Taste and add salt and more lime juice if needed. You should have about 2 cups (16 fl oz/500 ml). (The marinade can be made up to 2 days in advance and refrigerated.)

2 Place the pork cubes in a large lock-top plastic bag and pour in the marinade. Seal the bag closed, squish the marinade around the meat, and refrigerate for at least 4 hours, or overnight is better.

3 At least 30 minutes before you plan to begin grilling, remove the pork from the refrigerator. Discard the marinade. Do not pat the meat dry. This is one of the few times when you don't want it dry. If using wooden skewers, soak them in water for at least 30 minutes.

4 In a large pot, combine the sweet potato cubes with water to cover. Bring to a boil over high heat and cook for 5 minutes. Drain and let cool.

5 Prepare a charcoal or gas grill for direct grilling over high heat (page 16 or 18). Brush and oil the grill grate.

6 Alternately thread the pork and sweet potato cubes onto the skewers, leaving a little space between the cubes.

7 Place the skewers on the grill and cook until the pork and sweet potatoes are nicely grill-marked, about 5 minutes. Turn the skewers and cook for about 5 minutes longer. The pork should feel just firm to the touch (for medium), and the sweet potato cubes should be tender.

8 Transfer the skewers to a platter and let rest for about 5 minutes. Slide the pork and sweet potato cubes off the skewers onto the platter, and serve.

GOES GREAT WITH Coconut Rice (page 196); Grilled Veggies (page 201); Skillet Corn Bread (page 206)

How to grill the perfect
Pork Chops

The grilled pork chop is a classic. It pairs well with lots of different flavors and has plenty of flavor on its own. But it also can be the most leathery piece of meat you have ever tried to eat. That's because pork is generally bred to be fairly lean and folks overcook it. Here's how to grill pork chops so they are always irresistibly juicy.

GO THICK, NOT THIN Don't try to grill thin pork chops. Bread them and fry them, and they'll taste great. But if you put them on the grill, they will cook too fast and end up tough and flavorless. Buy chops that are at least ¾ to 1 inch (2 to 2.5 cm) thick. I prefer bone-in chops—a gracefully curved rib chop or a husky T-bone (center cut)—which cook more evenly and have more flavor than boneless chops.

BRINE, BRINE, BRINE Brining pork chops, even for a short time, provides a little wiggle room on doneness. If you are forgetful and cook the chop for a minute or two too long, the brine will help keep the meat moist. Check out the brine recipe on page 211. And remember to pat the chops dry with paper towels so they sear, rather than steam, on the grill.

WATCH THE HEAT Pork doesn't like high heat. Put a chop over a hot fire, and you'll end up with a tough piece of meat, even if you've brined it. Setting up your grill for indirect grilling is a good way to go. You can put a quick sear on both sides of the chop and then move it to the indirect-heat area for slower cooking.

GOES GREAT WITH Almost any type of grilled fruit rides nicely alongside a grilled pork chop—a triumph of sweet and savory. Plums and peaches are especially good additions to the plate. You could also serve these with a colorful Chopped Salad (page 204) and Skillet Corn Bread (page 206).

Brined Pork Chops
with Grilled Stone Fruit

6 bone-in pork chops, each
at least 1 inch (2.5 cm) thick

Basic Pork Brine (page 211)

6 ripe but slightly firm plums,
peaches, or nectarines, halved
and pitted

Canola oil for brushing

---

1 Place the pork chops in a large lock-top plastic bag and pour in the brine. Seal the bag closed, squish the brine around the chops, and refrigerate overnight.

2 At least 30 minutes before you plan to begin grilling, remove the chops from the refrigerator. Discard the brine, rinse the chops briefly in cold water, and pat dry with paper towels.

3 Prepare a charcoal or gas grill for indirect grilling over medium heat; the temperature inside the grill should be 350°–375°F (180°–190°C). If using charcoal, bank the lit coals on either side of the grill bed, leaving a strip in the center without heat, and place a drip pan in the center (page 16). If using gas, preheat the burners, then turn off 1 or more of the burners to create a cooler zone (page 19). Brush and oil the grill grate.

4 Place the pork chops on the grill over the direct-heat area and sear, turning once, until nicely grill-marked on both sides, 2–3 minutes on each side. Move the chops to the indirect-heat area, cover the grill, and cook until the chops are somewhat firm to the touch, about 15 minutes for medium, or until an instant-read thermometer inserted horizontally into the center of a chop away from bone registers 145°F (63°C).

5 Transfer the chops to a platter and let rest for 10 minutes. Meanwhile, brush both sides of the fruit halves with oil and grill over the direct-heat area until nicely grill-marked, about 2 minutes on each side. Serve the pork chops at once with the grilled fruit on the side.

SERVES 6

Pork Loin Chops
with Romesco Sauce and Grilled Onions

FOR THE ROMESCO SAUCE

½ cup (3 oz/90 g) roasted
red peppers

⅓ cup (2 oz/60 g) raw almonds

1 slice sourdough bread,
crust removed

2 cloves garlic

2 tablespoons red wine vinegar

½ teaspoon red pepper flakes

¼ cup (2 fl oz/60 ml) extra-
virgin olive oil

6 bone-in center-cut loin pork
chops, each about 10 oz (315 g)
and 1 inch (2.5 cm) thick

Kosher salt and freshly
ground pepper

Olive oil for brushing

12 green onions, trimmed
but left whole

SERVES 6

The Game Plan

- Make *romesco* sauce

- Remove pork from fridge;
  season and brush with oil

- Set up grill for direct grilling
  over medium heat

- Trim green onions; toss with
  oil and season with salt

- Grilling time: 10–12 minutes

- DON'T FORGET Bone-in
  chops will be juicier and
  more flavorful than boneless.

Romesco sauce goes well with most any grilled food. In fact, grill cooks should serve it more than they do. Paired here with pork chops and green onions, it ups the profile of the menu—it's good enough for company and easy enough for every day. Turn the green onions carefully so they don't slip through the grate.

1 To make the sauce, in a blender, combine the roasted peppers, almonds, bread, garlic, vinegar, and red pepper flakes and process until fairly smooth. With the machine running, slowly pour in the ¼ cup olive oil and process until the sauce emulsifies. (The sauce can be made 1 day in advance and refrigerated. Bring to room temperature before using.)

2 At least 30 minutes before you plan to begin grilling, remove the pork chops from the refrigerator. Season the chops generously on both sides with salt and pepper. Brush both sides with olive oil.

3 Prepare a charcoal or gas grill for direct grilling over medium heat (page 16 or 18). Brush and oil the grill grate.

4 Toss the green onions lightly with olive oil and sprinkle with salt. Place the chops on the grill directly over the fire and cook until nicely grill-marked, about 5 minutes. Turn the chops and add the green onions to the grill. Cook the chops until well marked and cooked to your liking, another 5–7 minutes for medium, or until an instant-read thermometer inserted horizontally into the center of a chop away from bone registers 145°F (63°C). Transfer the chops to a platter. Turn the green onions, and cook until tender and slightly wilted, about 2 minutes longer.

5 Place the green onions on the platter with the pork and serve at once, passing the sauce on the side.

GOES GREAT WITH Grilled Asparagus with Lemon Mayonnaise (page 166); Spinach and Bacon Salad (page 205); Garlic Bread (page 207)

Pork Chops
with Dueling Jams

6 bone-in rib pork chops,
each about 10 oz (315 g)
and 1¼ inches (3 cm) thick

Basic Pork Brine (page 211)

Bacon-Onion Jam (page 216)
for serving

Spicy Tomato Jam (page 215)
for serving

SERVES 6

The Game Plan

* Make both jams; refrigerate

* Make brine; brine chops for
  4 hours or up to overnight

* Remove chops from fridge
  and discard brine; rinse and
  pat dry

* Set up grill for direct grilling
  over 2 heat levels: high
  and medium

* Grilling time: 12–15 minutes

* DON'T FORGET First sear the
  chops over high heat and
  then finish cooking them
  over medium heat.

Here is a flavor explosion—reminiscent of a BLT, but better. Both jams are simple to make and are great not only with pork but also steak, chicken, or fish. You might want to double the recipes so you have them on hand in the refrigerator for when you need a quick fix for the dinner table.

1 Place the pork chops in a large lock-top plastic bag and pour in the brine. Seal the bag closed, squish the brine around the chops, and refrigerate for at least 4 hours, or overnight is better.

2 At least 30 minutes before you plan to begin grilling, remove the chops from the refrigerator. Discard the brine, rinse the chops briefly in cold water, and pat dry with paper towels.

3 Prepare a charcoal or gas grill for direct grilling over 2 levels of heat, one high and one medium (page 16 or 18). Brush and oil the grill grate.

4 Place the chops on the hottest part of the grill and cook, turning once, until nicely grill marked on both sides, 2–3 minutes on each side. Move the chops to the medium-heat section of the grill and continue to cook for another 4 minutes. Turn and continue to cook the chops for 6–8 minutes for medium, or until an instant-read thermometer inserted horizontally into the center of a chop away from bone registers 145°F (63°C).

5 Transfer the chops to a platter or individual plates and let rest for about 5 minutes. Place a dollop of each jam alongside each chop. Serve at once.

GOES GREAT WITH Smoky Grilled Potatoes (page 176); Vinegar-Braised Collard Greens (page 199); Buttermilk Biscuits (page 206)

Corn Bread–Stuffed Pork Chops

FOR THE CORN BREAD STUFFING

½ lb (250 g) bulk breakfast sausage

1 yellow onion, finely chopped

1 rib celery, finely chopped

2 cloves garlic, minced

1 tablespoon unsalted butter

1 teaspoon dried sage

2 cups (4 oz/125 g) cubed day-old corn bread, homemade (page 206) or store-bought

½ cup (4 fl oz/125 ml) apple cider

6 bone-in rib pork chops, each about 10 oz (315 g) and 1¼ inches (3 cm) thick

Kosher salt and freshly ground pepper

Canola oil for brushing

SERVES 6

The Game Plan

- Make stuffing
- Remove chops from fridge
- Set up grill for indirect grilling over medium heat
- Stuff chops; season and brush with oil
- Grilling time: about 18 minutes
- DON'T FORGET Be sure the stuffing reaches a safe temperature before you pull the chops off the grill.

This is about as Dixie as you can get. The key to success here is to buy good-quality country-style breakfast sausage and to make your own corn bread. When it comes time to grill the pork, combine direct and indirect heat for the best result: a nicely seared exterior and a juicy interior.

1 To make the stuffing, place a large frying pan over medium-high heat, and crumble in the sausage. Cook, stirring occasionally, until browned, about 4 minutes. Add the onion, celery, and garlic and cook, stirring occasionally, until the vegetables are wilted, about 4 minutes. Add the butter, sage, and corn bread cubes and stir and toss to combine evenly. Add the apple cider, mix well, and cook slowly until the corn bread begins to soften, about 3 minutes. Remove from the heat and let cool.

2 At least 30 minutes before you plan to begin grilling, remove the pork chops from the refrigerator.

3 Prepare a charcoal or gas grill for indirect grilling over medium heat; the temperature inside the grill should be 350°–375°F (180°–190°C). If using charcoal, bank the lit coals on either side of the grill bed, leaving a strip in the center without heat, and place a drip pan in the center (page 16). If using gas, preheat the burners, then turn off 1 or more of the burners to create a cooler zone (page 19). Brush and oil the grill grate.

4 Using a small, sharp knife, cut a horizontal slit about 3 inches (7.5 cm) long in the center of the fat-rimmed edge of each chop, cutting to within about 1 inch (2.5 cm) of the bone to create a nice pocket. Divide the stuffing evenly among the 6 chops; pack it into each pocket. Secure each pocket closed with a toothpick or kitchen string. Season the chops generously on both sides with salt and pepper. Brush the chops on both sides with the oil.

5 Place the chops on the grill over the direct-heat area, and sear, turning once, until nicely grill marked, about 4 minutes on each side. Move the chops to the indirect-heat area and cook for about another 10 minutes, or until an instant-read thermometer inserted into the center registers about 155°F (68°C).

6 Transfer to a platter and let rest for 10 minutes. Remove the toothpicks or snip the string and serve at once.

GOES GREAT WITH Vinegar-Braised Collard Greens (page 199); Cheesy Cauliflower Gratin (page 199); Watermelon Salad (page 203)

How to smoke the perfect
Baby Back Ribs

Ask a backyard grill master to name the holy grail of grilling, and the usual answer is perfect ribs. Frankly, even though ribs are simple to cook, folks come up with the oddest methods. First, don't ever parboil ribs that you'll be smoking. It makes them tough. Second, don't let the fire get too hot, or you'll end up with a batch of dry ribs.

REMOVE THE MEMBRANE Flip the ribs over so the backside is up. Slide a sharp knife under the corner of the thin membrane that covers the backside of the rack, then grab a corner of the membrane and rip it off (you can also use a paper towel to grab the membrane). The ribs will be easier to eat, will be infused with more flavor, and will cook more evenly.

STEAM-ROAST THE RIBS IN THE OVEN Loosely wrap the ribs in aluminum foil, add a little water to the package, and steam-roast the ribs in gentle heat in your oven for about an hour. This sets up an environment that guarantees moist ribs.

MIX YOUR WOOD CHIPS Don't use all hickory chips, which can give the ribs a bitter edge. Instead, use a mix of hickory and oak or a fruit wood.

USE BOTH INDIRECT AND DIRECT HEAT Cook the ribs over low indirect heat first, then, toward the end of cooking, move them to medium direct heat, and baste with the sauce.

DON'T OVERCOOK Some folks think that once the meat has pulled back from the bones 1 inch (2.5 cm) or so, the ribs are done. Wrong. On the competition circuit, ribs that look like that are called shiners because they are overcooked and dried out. A little bone showing is okay. The best way to tell when a rack of ribs is ready is to grab the long side with tongs, and if the ribs bend without resistance, they are done.

GOES GREAT WITH Serve these like they do in the South, with Smoky Baked Beans with Bacon (page 194), Vinegar-Braised Collard Greens (page 199), and Skillet Cornbread (page 206).

BBQ Baby Back Ribs

2 racks baby back ribs, about
3 lb (1.5 kg) each

2–3 tablespoons mustard
of your choice

All-Purpose BBQ Rub (page 208)

About 2 cups wood chips,
soaked in water for 30 minutes

Classic BBQ Sauce (page 212),
or 2 cups (16 fl oz/500 ml) of
your favorite BBQ sauce

About 2 tablespoons honey

1 Preheat the oven to 250°F (120°C). Remove the membrane from the back of each rack (page 94) and trim off any excess fat. Brush the mustard on both sides of the racks and sprinkle the rub on both sides. Gently pat the rub into the mustard. Place the ribs, side by side, on a large piece of aluminum foil and loosely wrap the ribs. Set on a rimmed baking sheet. Unwrap one corner and pour in ¼ cup (2 fl oz/60 ml) water; reseal the package. Bake the ribs in the oven for 1 hour.

2 Prepare a charcoal or gas grill for smoking over low heat (page 17 or 19); the temperature of the grill should be 200°–250°F (95°–120°C). If using charcoal, bank the lit coals on either side of the grill bed, leaving a strip in the center without heat. Place a drip pan in the center strip and fill the pan with water. Add about 1 cup of the wood chips to the fire just before grilling. If using gas, fill the smoker box with about 1 cup of the wood chips, then preheat the grill. Turn off 1 or more burners to create a cooler zone. Brush and oil the grill grate.

3 Remove the ribs from the oven. Unwrap the ribs and discard the foil. Place the ribs over the indirect-heat area of the grill, cover the grill, and smoke for 1 hour, adding the remaining wood chips after about 30 minutes.

4 If using a charcoal grill, ready some coals to raise the temperature of the fire to medium, then uncover the grill and add the hot coals. If using a gas grill, uncover the grill and raise the heat to medium. Move the ribs, meat side down, to the direct-heat area of the grill and brush with the BBQ sauce. Cook for 5 minutes, then turn the ribs and brush the bone side with sauce. Continue to cook for 20 minutes, turning and basting with the sauce every 5 minutes. On the last turn, drizzle the honey on the meaty side of the racks.

5 Transfer the racks to a cutting board and let rest for about 10 minutes. Cut the racks into individual ribs, pile them on a platter, and serve at once with the remaining sauce.

SERVES 4

Baby Back Ribs
with Asian-Style Glaze

2 racks baby back ribs,
about 3 lb (1.5 kg) each

Kosher salt and freshly
ground pepper

¼ cup (2 fl oz/60 ml)
rice vinegar

1 jalapeño chile, thinly
sliced into rings

Asian-Style Glaze (page 211)

¼ cup (⅓ oz/10 g) finely
chopped fresh cilantro

SERVES 4

The Game Plan

- Season ribs, wrap in foil, and bake for 1 hour

- Make glaze

- Set up grill for indirect grilling over medium heat

- Grilling time: about 1½ hours

- Brush with glaze during last 20 minutes of cooking

- Let racks rest, then slice

- DON'T FORGET Watch the ribs closely after you start brushing on the glaze; if they begin to burn, move them to a cooler part of the grill.

Asian cooks were slathering a sweet-hot glaze on ribs long before anyone in America mixed up the first BBQ sauce, so I decided to borrow some classic flavors from Asia to create this glaze. It is also good brushed on pork tenderloin and boneless pork chops.

1 Preheat the oven to 325°F (165°C). Remove the thin membrane from the back of each rack (page 94) and trim off any excess fat. Generously sprinkle the racks on both sides with salt and pepper. Place each rack on a sheet of aluminum foil and set on a rimmed baking sheet. Divide the vinegar and chile rings evenly between the racks, then wrap the foil around the racks and seal loosely. Bake the ribs in the oven for 1 hour.

2 About 30 minutes before the ribs are ready, prepare a charcoal or gas grill for indirect grilling over medium heat; the temperature inside the grill should be 350°–375°F (180°–190°C). If using charcoal, bank the lit coals on either side of the grill bed, leaving a strip in the center without heat, and place a drip pan in the center (page 16). If using gas, preheat the burners, then turn off 1 or more of the burners to create a cooler zone (page 19). Brush and oil the grill grate.

3 When the ribs are ready, remove them from the oven. Remove and discard the foil along with the vinegar, chile rings, and any fat that has accumulated. Place the ribs, meat side down, on the grill over the indirect-heat area, cover the grill, and cook for 1 hour.

4 If using a charcoal grill, ready some coals to raise the temperature of the fire to medium, then uncover the grill and add the hot coals. If using a gas grill, uncover the grill and raise the heat to medium. Move the ribs, meat side down, to the direct-heat area of the grill and cook until nicely seared, about 4 minutes. Turn and cook until nicely seared on the bone side, about 4 minutes longer. Start brushing the ribs with the glaze every 5 minutes, turning each time. Continue to cook for about 20 minutes, turning and basting with the glaze every 5 minutes. If the glaze begins to burn, reduce the heat if using a gas grill or move to a cooler part of the grill if using a charcoal grill.

5 Transfer the racks to a cutting board and let rest for about 10 minutes. Cut the racks into individual ribs and pile them on a platter. Sprinkle with the cilantro and serve hot, warm, or at room temperature.

GOES GREAT WITH Coconut Rice (page 196); Asian-Style Slaw (page 203); Cucumber Salad (page 203)

Bourbon-Marmalade Spareribs

3 tablespoons All-Purpose
BBQ Rub (page 208)

Bourbon-Orange Marinade
(page 211)

3 racks pork spareribs, about
3 lb (1.5 kg) each, cracked (but
not cut apart) by the butcher

SERVES 6

The Game Plan

- Make rub; season ribs

- Make marinade; marinate
  ribs 8 hours or up to overnight

- Remove ribs from fridge;
  reserve marinade

- Put ribs in foil packets

- Set up grill for indirect grilling
  over medium heat

- Grilling time: about 1½ hours

- Heat reserved marinade
  and brush on ribs during
  last 10 minutes

- Let racks rest, then slice

- DON'T FORGET The marinade
  has sugar in it, so check the
  ribs every so often to make
  sure they aren't burning.

This unusual mix of bourbon, with its vanilla and honey overtones, and slightly bittersweet orange marmalade is guaranteed to become one of your go-to recipes. The marinade does double duty here, becoming a basting sauce toward the end of cooking.

1 To ensure the racks cook evenly, carefully cut off the pork flank steak (that hunk of meat on the back of each rack) and reserve it for another use. Remove the membrane from the back of each rack (page 94). Sprinkle the ribs on both sides with the BBQ rub. Slice each rack in half crosswise. Place all the ribs in a large lock-top plastic bag.

2 Pour the marinade over the ribs. Seal the bag closed, squish the marinade around the ribs, and refrigerate for at least 8 hours, or overnight is better. At least 1 hour before you plan to begin grilling, take the ribs out of the refrigerator and remove from the marinade; reserve the marinade. Make aluminum foil packets containing 2 rib rack halves, making 3 packets total.

3 Prepare a charcoal or gas grill for indirect grilling over medium heat; the temperature inside the grill should be 350°–375°F (180°–190°C). If using charcoal, bank the lit coals on either side of the grill bed, leaving a strip in the center without heat, and place a drip pan in the center (page 16). If using gas, preheat the burners, then turn off 1 or more of the burners to create a cooler zone (page 19). Brush and oil the grill grate.

4 Place the rib packets on the grill over the indirect-heat area and cook for about 1½ hours, adding more coals as needed if using a charcoal grill. Check after 45 minutes to make sure the ribs are not burning. If they are, reduce the heat if using a gas grill or move to a cooler area if using a charcoal grill.

5 Place the reserved marinade in a small saucepan, bring to a boil over medium-high heat, and boil for at least 1 minute. Reduce the heat to medium and simmer until slightly thickened, about 10 minutes.

6 Remove the ribs from the foil packets and place them over the direct-heat side of the grill, meat side down. Grill, brushing them with the marinade and turning them once or twice, until glazed and fork-tender, 8–10 minutes.

7 Transfer to a cutting board and let rest for about 10 minutes. Cut the racks into individual ribs, pile them on a platter, and serve at once.

GOES GREAT WITH Grilled Corn with Lime Butter (page 165); Mac and Cheese (page 196); Chopped Salad (page 204)

Coffee-Rubbed Pork Roast

FOR THE COFFEE RUB

1 tablespoon freshly ground
dark-roast coffee

1 teaspoon instant
espresso powder

1 teaspoon unsweetened
cocoa powder

1 teaspoon demerara
or turbinado sugar

Kosher salt and freshly
ground pepper

1 boneless pork loin roast,
about 2½ lb (1.25 kg)

Coffee BBQ Sauce
(page 213) for serving

SERVES 6–8

The Game Plan

- Make rub; season pork;
  let stand 30 minutes

- Make BBQ sauce; refrigerate

- Set up grill for indirect grilling
  over medium heat

- Grilling time: 1–1¼ hours

- Let pork rest, then slice

- DON'T FORGET Let the pork
  rest for a good 15 minutes
  before slicing it.

In addition to being the perfect morning beverage, coffee is an interesting flavoring for pork (and beef, too). Its distinct flavor is emphasized twice in this recipe: in a rub, which has the added bonus of cocoa powder, and in a sauce laced with cumin, jalapeño, and garlic. If you've never cooked with coffee before, this is a good place to start.

1 To make the rub, in a jar, combine the coffee, espresso powder, cocoa powder, sugar, 1 teaspoon salt, and 1 teaspoon pepper. Cover tightly and shake well to combine. Rub the pork loin all over with the rub. Let stand at room temperature for at least 30 minutes.

2 Prepare a charcoal or gas grill for indirect grilling over medium heat; the temperature inside the grill should be 350°–375°F (180°–190°C). If using charcoal, bank the lit coals on either side of the grill bed, leaving a strip in the center without heat, and place a drip pan in the center (page 16). If using gas, preheat the burners, then turn off 1 or more of the burners to create a cooler zone (page 19). Brush and oil the grill grate.

3 Place the pork loin on the grill over the indirect-heat area and cook for 1–1¼ hours for medium, or until an instant-read thermometer inserted into the thickest part of the roast registers 145°F (63°C).

4 Transfer the pork loin to a cutting board, tent with aluminum foil, and let rest for 15 minutes. Meanwhile, warm the BBQ sauce. Slice the pork, arrange the slices on a platter, and serve at once, passing the sauce alongside.

GOES GREAT WITH Grilled Romaine Salad (page 170); Smoky Baked Beans with Bacon (page 194); Buttermilk Biscuits (page 206)

Cuban Sandwiches
with Slow-Smoked Pork Loin

½ cup (4 fl oz/125 ml) sour orange juice or ¼ cup (2 fl oz/ 60 ml) *each* fresh orange juice and fresh lime juice, combined

1 boneless pork loin roast, about 3 lb (1.5 kg)

5 cloves garlic, finely chopped

1 teaspoon cumin

1 teaspoon dried oregano

Kosher salt and freshly ground pepper

About 8 cups wood chips, soaked in water for 30 minutes

8 hoagie or soft French rolls, split

Yellow mustard for spreading

½ lb (250 g) ham, thinly sliced

Dill pickle chips for serving

½ lb (250 g) provolone or Swiss cheese, sliced

SERVES 8

The Game Plan

- Inject pork with orange juice

- Make rub; season pork; refrigerate for 24 hours

- Remove pork from fridge

- Soak wood chips; set up grill for smoking over medium heat

- Grilling time: about 1 hour

- Assemble sandwiches; heat on grill

- DON'T FORGET Finish the sandwiches on the grill for extra-smoky flavor.

Although hot sandwiches prepared in a fancy electric press are all the rage today, the standard for me will always be the venerable pork-intensive *cubano*. Cuban sandwiches traditionally call for slow-roasted pork shoulder, but a smoked pork loin cooks more quickly and makes a sandwich that's just as tasty.

1 Load a marinade injector with the orange juice and inject the juice into the pork in several places. In a small bowl, stir together the garlic, cumin, oregano, 1½ teaspoons salt, and ½ teaspoon pepper. Rub the mixture evenly over the pork loin. Place the loin in a large lock-top plastic bag, seal the bag closed, and refrigerate for 24 hours.

2 At least 30 minutes before you plan to start grilling, remove the pork loin from the refrigerator, and remove it from the plastic bag.

3 Prepare a charcoal or gas grill for smoking over medium heat (page 17 or 19); the temperature inside the grill should be 350°–375°F (180°–190°C). If using charcoal, bank the lit coals on either side of the grill bed, leaving a strip in the center without heat. Place a drip pan in the center and fill the pan with water. Add half of the wood chips to the fire just before grilling. If using gas, fill the smoker box with wood chips, then preheat the grill. Turn off 1 or more burners to create a cooler zone. Brush and oil the grill grate.

4 Place the pork on the grill over the direct-heat area and sear, turning as needed, until nicely browned on all sides, about 10 minutes. Move the pork roast to the indirect-heat area, cover, and cook for about 1 hour, or until an instant-read thermometer inserted into the thickest part of the loin registers 145°F (63°C), adding the remaining wood chips after about 30 minutes.

5 Transfer the pork loin to a cutting board, tent with aluminum foil, and let rest for about 10 minutes. If using a charcoal grill, spread the coals out evenly over the fire bed. If using a gas grill, turn the burners to high.

6 Coat the cut sides of the rolls with the mustard. Evenly divide the ham among the rolls, and then top with some of the pickles. Slice the pork thinly, and place some of the pork slices over the pickles. (You will have leftover pork; it will keep in the refrigerator for 1 week.) Top with the cheese slices. Place the sandwiches on the grill over direct heat. Using a long spatula, press down on each sandwich until the cheese melts, 2–3 minutes. Serve at once.

GOES GREAT WITH Southwestern Bean Salad (page 195); Creamy Coleslaw (page 202); Tortilla chips and Smoky Tomato Salsa (page 214)

Carolina-Style Pulled Pork

1 bone-in pork shoulder,
4–5 lb (2–2.5 kg)

¾ cup (6 fl oz/180 ml)
apple cider

½ cup (4 oz/125 g) sugar

¼ cup (2 oz/60 g) kosher salt,
plus salt as needed

2 tablespoons Worcestershire
sauce

1 tablespoon hot-pepper sauce

Freshly ground pepper

5 lb (2.5 kg) applewood or
hickory chips, or a mixture,
soaked in water for 30 minutes

Classic BBQ Sauce (page 212)
for serving

Lexington-Style Dip
(page 212) for serving

10–12 soft hamburger buns

SERVES 10–12

The Game Plan

- Make BBQ sauce and
  Lexington dip; refrigerate

- Make flavoring for injector;
  inject pork with flavoring

- Soak wood chips; set up
  smoker or grill for smoking
  over low heat

- Grilling time: about 10 hours

- Wrap pork in foil after 4 hours;
  return to grill or finish in oven

- Let pork cool, then shred

- DON'T FORGET This is a
  long, slow process, so be
  patient—it's worth the wait.

Excuse me for bragging, but I am a North Carolina boy and you are about to learn how to make the finest pulled pork on the planet. You start by injecting the meat with a cider-based flavoring, and then you cook it nice and slow. I prefer to use both the grill and the oven for ease.

1 At least 1 hour before you plan to begin cooking, remove the pork from the refrigerator. In a jar, combine the apple cider, sugar, salt, Worcestershire sauce, hot-pepper sauce, and ½ cup (4 fl oz/125 ml) warm water. Cover and shake the jar vigorously until the sugar and salt have dissolved. Load a marinade injector with the apple cider mixture, and inject the mixture into the pork in several places. Season the pork on all sides with salt and pepper.

2 Prepare a smoker (page 8) or a charcoal or gas grill for smoking over low heat (page 17 or 19); the temperature of the grill should be 200°–250°F (95°–120°C). If using charcoal, bank the lit coals on either side of the grill bed, leaving a strip in the center without heat. Place a drip pan in the center strip and fill the pan with water. Add a handful of the wood chips to the fire just before grilling. If using gas, fill the smoker box with wood chips, then preheat the grill. Turn off 1 or more of the burners to create a cooler zone. Brush and oil the grill grate.

3 Place the pork on the grill over the indirect-heat area, cover, and smoke for a total of about 4 hours, adding additional wood chips every 30 minutes or so and more coals as needed if using charcoal.

4 After 4 hours, remove the pork and double wrap it in aluminum foil. You can put it back on the grill and cook it slowly for another 6 hours (I don't recommend this if you're using charcoal), or you can place it in a roasting pan in a 250°F (120°C) oven for an additional 6 hours. The pork is ready when you can easily slide out the bone with a pair of tongs.

5 Transfer the pork to a cutting board and let cool for about 30 minutes. Remove any fat cap. Using 2 forks, pull and shred all the meat. Sprinkle a little salt over the pork and add about ½ cup (4 fl oz/125 ml) BBQ sauce and toss to blend. Pile the meat on a platter and put out the buns, remaining BBQ sauce, and the Lexington-style dip. Then dig in.

GOES GREAT WITH Smoky Baked Beans with Bacon (page 194); Potato Salad (page 195); Lexington-Style Slaw (page 202)

How to grill the perfect
BBQ Chicken

Classic barbecued chicken doesn't begin with boneless, skinless chicken breasts. You have to have bones to develop great flavor. Nor do you want your chicken to be burnt on the outside and raw on the inside, which is what happens to too many cooks. Here is how to fix those problems and more.

BRINE THE BIRD Brining adds some flavor, but more importantly, it ensures a moist result. It also makes the timing a little less fussy. If you get distracted and the chicken pieces stay on the grill 5 minutes too long, it's no big deal.

PAT IT DRY Don't forget this step before you throw the chicken on the grill. Patting the pieces dry with paper towels helps the surface caramelize, which is the slight charring that takes place once the meat hits the heat. If the surface is moist from a brine or marinade, it will steam rather than sear, and you'll miss out on that tasty caramelization.

USE TWO HEAT LEVELS The chicken gets a quick sear over direct heat, but most of the grilling is done over indirect heat. That lower heat helps to develop an intense barbecue flavor.

SAUCE IT UP Using indirect heat allows you to brush the BBQ sauce on the chicken earlier without fear of the sauce burning. That extra brushing time means you'll end up with more of the signature tangy flavor of good barbecue.

GOES GREAT WITH Honestly, barbecued chicken will go well with just about any side you can think of. Some of my all-time favorites: Grilled Corn with Lime Butter (page 165), Potato Salad (page 195), Mac and Cheese (page 196), and Skillet Corn Bread (page 206).

Classic BBQ Chicken

1 chicken, 4 lb (2 kg), neck
and giblets removed,
cut into 4 pieces

Basic Poultry Brine (page 211)

Freshly ground pepper and
granulated garlic for sprinkling

2 cups (16 fl oz/500 ml) Classic
BBQ Sauce (page 212)

---

1 Put the chicken pieces in a large lock-top plastic bag and pour in the brine. Seal the bag closed, squish the brine around the chicken, and refrigerate overnight.

2 At least 30 minutes before you plan to begin grilling, remove the chicken from the brine and discard the brine. Rinse the chicken pieces briefly and pat dry with paper towels. Lightly sprinkle on all sides with pepper and granulated garlic.

3 Prepare a charcoal or gas grill for indirect grilling over medium heat; the temperature inside the grill should be about 350°F (180°C). If using charcoal, bank the lit coals on either side of the grill bed, leaving a strip in the center without heat, and place a drip pan in the center (page 16). If using gas, preheat the burners, then turn off 1 or more of the burners to create a cooler zone (page 19). Brush and oil the grill grate.

4 Place the chicken pieces on the grill over the direct-heat area and sear, turning once, for 2 minutes on each side. Move the chicken pieces to the indirect-heat area, cover the grill, and cook for 30 minutes. Now, start brushing the chicken with the BBQ sauce, turning and brushing the pieces every 5 minutes, for about 15 minutes longer. The chicken is ready when it is firm to the touch and the juices run clear when a thigh or breast is pierced with a knife tip.

5 Transfer the chicken pieces to a platter and serve at once. Pass the remaining sauce at the table.

SERVES 4

Spicy Chicken Wings
with Blue Cheese Dip

3 lb (1.5 kg) chicken wings, tips removed

3 tablespoons canola oil

2 tablespoons All-Purpose BBQ Rub (page 208)

½ cup (4 oz/125 g) unsalted butter

6 cloves garlic, minced

½ cup (4 fl oz/125 ml) hot-pepper sauce

1 tablespoon distilled white vinegar

Blue Cheese Dip (page 217) for serving

Celery sticks for serving

SERVES 6–8 AS
AN APPETIZER

The Game Plan

- Make rub; season chicken; refrigerate overnight

- Make blue cheese dip; refrigerate

- Make hot sauce

- Set up grill for direct grilling over high heat

- Grilling time: 15–20 minutes

- Toss wings in hot sauce

- DON'T FORGET You want to get a nice char on the wings, but if they are burning too quickly, move them to a cooler area of the grill.

A while ago, I gave up frying chicken wings in favor of grilling them. This recipe is in the style of the famed buffalo wings, with a nice bonus of some charred smokiness from the grill. Once you try these, you'll agree that the cook at the Anchor Bar in Buffalo, New York, birthplace of the buffalo wing, should have grilled them, too.

1 In a large bowl, combine the wings and oil. Toss until the wings are evenly coated. Sprinkle the BBQ rub over the wings and toss again to coat evenly. Cover and refrigerate overnight.

2 At least 30 minutes before you are ready to begin grilling, remove the wings from the refrigerator. In a large frying pan over medium heat, melt the butter. Add the garlic and cook, stirring, until fragrant and tender, about 2 minutes. Pour in the hot sauce and vinegar, stir well, remove from the heat, and set the pan aside at room temperature.

3 Prepare a charcoal or gas grill for direct grilling over high heat (page 16 or 18). Brush and oil the grill grate.

4 Place the chicken wings on the grill directly over the fire and cook, turning frequently, until they are nicely browned on all sides, have some char, and are tender, 15–20 minutes.

5 Transfer the wings to the hot sauce in the frying pan, place the pan over low heat, and toss the wings in the sauce to coat evenly. Let the wings and the sauce marry for about 5 minutes.

6 Transfer the wings to a platter and pour any remaining sauce in the pan over the top. Serve with the blue cheese dip and celery sticks.

GOES GREAT WITH Grilled Pizza Margherita (page 183); Mac and Cheese (page 196); Chopped Salad (page 204)

Caribbean Jerk Chicken
with Grilled Pineapple Salsa

6 whole chicken legs

Caribbean Jerk Seasoning
(page 209)

Grilled Pineapple Salsa
(page 215) for serving

SERVES 6

The Game Plan

- Make seasoning; season chicken; refrigerate overnight
- Remove chicken from fridge
- Set up grill for indirect grilling over medium heat
- Make pineapple salsa
- Grilling time: about 35 minutes
- DON'T FORGET The best way to test for doneness is with an instant-read thermometer, so have yours handy.

Many people believe that the jerk seasoning of the Caribbean is too spicy to handle. But made correctly, jerk chicken is a deeply flavored dish with the perfect amount of heat. I like to use whole chicken legs because they stay on the grill long enough to develop an intense flavor. The pineapple salsa adds a cooling note and a bit of sweetness.

1 Place the chicken legs on a platter and coat evenly on all sides with the jerk seasoning. Cover and refrigerate for at least 8 hours or up to overnight.

2 At least 30 minutes before you are ready to begin grilling, remove the chicken from the refrigerator.

3 Prepare a charcoal or gas grill for indirect grilling over medium heat; the temperature inside the grill should be 350°–375°F (180°–190°C). If using charcoal, bank the lit coals on either side of the grill bed, leaving a strip in the center without heat, and place a drip pan in the center (page 16). If using gas, preheat the burners, then turn off 1 or more of the burners to create a cooler zone (page 19). Brush and oil the grill grate.

4 Make the pineapple salsa using the direct-heat area of the grill. (Or make the salsa up to 2 days in advance and refrigerate until ready to use.)

5 Place the chicken legs on the grill over the direct-heat area and sear, turning once, until nicely browned on both sides, about 2 minutes on each side. Move the chicken legs to the indirect-heat area and cook until firm to the touch and an instant-read thermometer inserted into the thickest part of the thigh away from bone registers 170°F (77°C), about 30 minutes.

6 Transfer the chicken to a platter and let rest for 10 minutes. Serve at once. Pass the salsa at the table.

GOES GREAT WITH Grilled Summer Squash with Fresh Mint Vinaigrette (page 169); Coconut Rice (page 196); Watermelon Salad (page 203)

Honey-Sesame Glazed Chicken Wings

3 lb (1.5 kg) chicken wings, tips removed

¼ cup (2 fl oz/60 ml) canola oil

2 tablespoons *shichimi togarashi* spice blend or lemon pepper

¾ cup (6 fl oz/180 ml) sweet hot chile sauce

¼ cup (2 fl oz/60 ml) teriyaki sauce, homemade (page 213) or store-bought

2 tablespoons honey

2 tablespoons Asian sesame oil

Juice of 1 lime

2 tablespoons sesame seeds, toasted (optional)

SERVES 6–8 AS AN APPETIZER

The Game Plan

- Coat wings with oil and season with spice blend

- Set up grill for direct grilling over high heat

- Make glaze

- Grilling time: 15–20 minutes

- Coat wings in glaze

- DON'T FORGET It's better to glaze the wings after you've grilled them so the glaze won't burn on the grill.

Whether it's Super Bowl Sunday or you're just having a party, grill up a batch of these wings. Sweet, spicy, and tangy—they bring together some of Japan's greatest flavors into one memorable dish. If you are new to Japanese *shichimi togarashi,* a blend of chile, sesame seeds, seaweed, citrus rind, and other ingredients, I guarantee it will become a staple in your seasoning arsenal.

1 In a large bowl, combine the wings and oil and toss until the wings are evenly coated. Sprinkle the *shichimi togarashi* spice blend over the chicken wings and toss again to coat evenly. This is not a heavy coating. Set aside at room temperature for about 30 minutes.

2 Prepare a charcoal or gas grill for direct grilling over high heat (page 16 or 18). Brush and oil the grill grate.

3 To make the glaze, in a small saucepan, stir together the chile sauce, teriyaki sauce, honey, and sesame oil. Place over low heat and bring to a gentle simmer, stirring. Remove from the heat and let cool slightly. Stir in the lime juice. Reserve at room temperature.

4 Place the chicken wings on the grill and cook, turning frequently, until they are nicely browned on all sides, have some char, and are nice and tender, 15–20 minutes.

5 Transfer the wings to a large bowl, pour the glaze over them, and toss to coat evenly. Let sit for about 5 minutes to allow the flavors to meld, then transfer to a platter, sprinkle with the sesame seeds, if using, and serve at once.

GOES GREAT WITH Grilled Pineapple Skewers with Chile-Lime Salt (page 179); Coconut Rice (page 196); Asian-Style Slaw (page 203)

Marinated Duck Breasts
with Orange Glaze

FOR THE MARINADE

Grated zest and juice of
1 large orange

⅓ cup (3 fl oz/80 ml) dry sherry

⅓ cup (3 fl oz/80 ml) bourbon

1 tablespoon Worcestershire
sauce

2 tablespoons grated shallot

Kosher salt and freshly
ground pepper

4 boneless, skin-on duck breast
halves, about 12 oz (340 g) each

1 cup (10 oz/315 g) orange
marmalade, gently heated
until liquid

SERVES 4

The Game Plan

- Make marinade; marinate
  duck overnight

- Remove duck from fridge;
  discard marinade; pat dry

- Set up grill for direct grilling
  over medium heat

- Grilling time: 11–13 minutes

- Brush with marmalade during
  last 5–7 minutes

- DON'T FORGET Duck is fatty,
  so be prepared to deal with
  flare-ups.

In culinary history, duck with orange has always been considered haute cuisine. Add your grill and a little bourbon, and you'll make new culinary history in short order. Remember, always cook duck breast medium-rare for the best flavor and texture, and grill it skin side down for most of the cooking time to ensure the skin is crispy.

1 To make the marinade, in a small bowl, stir together the orange zest and juice, sherry, bourbon, Worcestershire sauce, shallot, ¼ teaspoon salt, and a few grinds of pepper.

2 Place the duck breast halves in a large lock-top plastic bag and pour in the marinade. Seal the bag closed, squish the marinade around the duck, and refrigerate overnight. Be sure to turn the bag over several times while the duck is marinating.

3 At least 30 minutes before you are ready to begin grilling, remove the duck from the refrigerator. Discard the marinade and pat the breast halves dry with paper towels.

4 Prepare a charcoal or gas grill for direct grilling over medium heat (page 16 or 18). Brush and oil the grill grate. Any time you are grilling duck, you are likely to have a flare-up, so if using charcoal, have a spray bottle full of cold water handy to douse the flames.

5 Place the duck breasts, skin side down, on the grill directly over the fire and cook until the skin is nicely browned and crispy, about 6 minutes. If you get flare-ups, move the breasts away from the flames. If using charcoal, use your water bottle to extinguish them (but be careful—the steam created from the water can cause burns). The skin should have a nice golden char and not be burnt black. Turn the breasts and brush with the marmalade. Cook for another 5–7 minutes for a perfect medium-rare duck breast.

6 Transfer the duck breasts to a platter, brush once again with the marmalade, and let rest for about 5 minutes. Serve at once with any remaining marmalade on the side.

GOES GREAT WITH Herbed Rice Pilaf (page 197); Spinach and Bacon Salad (page 205); Buttery Dinner Rolls (page 207)

Chicken, Shrimp, and Sausage Paella

¼ teaspoon saffron threads

6 bone-in, skin-on
chicken thighs

Kosher salt and freshly
ground pepper

1 Spanish-style chorizo sausage

¼ cup (2 fl oz/60 ml) olive oil

3 tomatoes, finely chopped

1 yellow onion, finely chopped

4 cloves garlic, minced

1 tablespoon chopped
fresh thyme

½ teaspoon smoked paprika

1 cup (7 oz/220 g) short-grain
paella rice such as bomba

4 cups (32 fl oz/1 l) low-sodium
chicken broth, or as needed

1 jar (7 oz/220 g) roasted
red peppers, drained

½ cup (2½ oz/75 g) fresh
or frozen English peas

1 lb (500 g) shrimp in the shell,
deveined (see page 154)

Chopped fresh flat-leaf parsley
leaves for garnish

1 lemon, cut into 6 wedges

SERVES 6

The Game Plan

- Set up grill for direct grilling
  over high heat

- Prep all your ingredients;
  layer in pan as directed

- Grilling time: about 1 hour

- DON'T FORGET Resist the
  urge to stir the paella as it
  cooks—you should have
  a nice crust on the bottom.

A grill is perfect for cooking paella: You first sear the chicken and chorizo, then sauté the vegetables in the pan, building layers of flavor. Once they're done, the rest of the ingredients are added and the paella cooks away on the grill, giving you plenty of time to open a bottle of good Spanish wine.

1 In a small bowl, add the saffron threads to ¼ cup (2 fl oz/60 ml) hot water and set aside. Prepare a charcoal or gas grill for direct grilling over high heat (page 16 or 18). Brush and oil the grill grate.

2 Season the chicken with salt and pepper. Slice the chorizo. Place a 15-inch (38-cm) paella pan on the grill directly over the fire, let it heat for a few minutes, and then add the oil. When the oil is hot, add the chicken thighs, skin side down, and sear, turning once, until nicely browned on both sides, about 5 minutes on each side. Add the chorizo and cook, turning often, until browned, about 5 minutes. Transfer the chicken and chorizo to a platter.

3 Add the tomatoes, onion, garlic, thyme, and paprika to the oil remaining in the pan and cook, stirring often, until softened, about 5 minutes. Season with salt and pepper. Stir in the rice and cook, stirring, until lightly toasted, 2–3 minutes. Pour in 2 cups (16 fl oz/500 ml) of the broth and bring to a boil. Cover the grill and cook for about 10 minutes.

4 Arrange the reserved chicken and chorizo evenly over the rice, and then nestle the chicken into the rice. Add 1 cup (8 fl oz/250 ml) of the broth, re-cover the grill, and cook for another 20 minutes. Cut the roasted peppers into strips. Top the rice evenly with the peas, roasted pepper strips, and shrimp. If the rice looks dry, add as much of the remaining broth as needed to moisten. Re-cover and cook until the shrimp are opaque, 7–10 minutes.

5 Remove the paella from the grill and sprinkle with the parsley. Serve at once with the lemon wedges.

GOES GREAT WITH Grilled Veggies (page 201); Chopped Salad (page 204); Garlic Bread (page 207)

Cumin-Crusted Chicken Thighs
with Grilled Tomatillo Salsa

8 bone-in, skin-on
chicken thighs

¼ cup (2 fl oz/60 ml) canola oil

¼ cup (1 oz/30 g) Cumin Crust
Rub (page 208)

FOR THE TOMATILLO SALSA

7 large tomatillos, papery husks
removed, and cut in half

1 jalapeño chile, halved
lengthwise and seeded

¼ cup (2 fl oz/60 ml) fresh
lime juice

1 tablespoon olive oil

½ cup (¾ oz/20 g) chopped
fresh cilantro

Kosher salt

SERVES 4–8

The Game Plan

- Make rub; coat chicken with
  oil and season with rub

- Set up grill for indirect grilling
  over medium heat

- Make tomatillo salsa

- Grilling time: 20–30 minutes

- DON'T FORGET Try to turn
  the thighs only once so they
  develop nice grill marks.

This is an amazing recipe. Cumin, smoked paprika, and other
bold spices in the rub come together with a chunky salsa of
tomatillos, chile, lime, and cilantro to deliver an explosion of
flavors that complement the chicken. If you have cumin haters
in the family, this recipe could just change their minds.

1 In a large bowl, combine the chicken thighs and oil. Toss to coat the
thighs evenly. Transfer the thighs to a platter and sprinkle evenly on all
sides with the cumin rub. Set aside at room temperature.

2 Prepare a charcoal or gas grill for indirect grilling over medium heat;
the temperature inside the grill should be 350°–375°F (180°–190°C). If using
charcoal, bank the lit coals on either side of the grill bed, leaving a strip in
the center without heat, and place a drip pan in the center (page 16). If using
gas, preheat the burners, then turn off 1 or more of the burners to create a
cooler zone (page 19). Brush and oil the grill grate.

3 To make the salsa, place the tomatillos and chile over the direct-heat
area of the grill. (You'll probably need a grill screen for the chile or you'll
lose it through the grate.) Cook, turning as needed, until well charred on
all sides, about 3 minutes. Transfer the tomatillos and chile to a blender, add
the lime juice and oil, and pulse until combined but still chunky. Transfer
to a bowl, fold in the cilantro, and season with salt. You should have about
2 cups (16 fl oz/500 ml). (The salsa can be made up to 1 week in advance
and refrigerated. Bring to room temperature before serving.)

4 Place the thighs, meaty side down, over the indirect-heat area of the
grill. Cook, turning once, until the thighs are nicely grill-marked on both
sides and firm to the touch and an instant-read thermometer inserted into
the thickest part of the thigh away from bone registers 170°F (77°C),
10–15 minutes on each side.

5 Transfer the thighs to a platter and let rest for 10 minutes. Serve at once
with the tomatillo salsa.

GOES GREAT WITH Mexican Rice (page 197); Spinach and Bacon Salad
(page 205); Skillet Corn Bread (page 206)

Tandoori-Style Chicken Kebabs

FOR THE TANDOORI MARINADE

2 cups (1 lb/500 g) plain whole-milk yogurt

2 tablespoons fresh lemon juice

2 tablespoons peeled and minced fresh ginger

4 cloves garlic, minced

1 teaspoon *each* ground coriander and ground turmeric

½ teaspoon *each* saffron threads, ground cumin, and cayenne pepper

Kosher salt and freshly ground black pepper

8 boneless, skinless chicken thighs

6–12 metal or wooden skewers

1 small red onion, thinly sliced and separated into rings

¼ cup (⅓ oz/10 g) chopped fresh cilantro

SERVES 6

The Game Plan

- Make marinade; cube chicken; marinate overnight

- Remove chicken from fridge and discard marinade; soak skewers if using wooden

- Set up grill for direct grilling over high heat

- Thread chicken onto skewers

- Grilling time: about 10 minutes

- DON'T FORGET These cook quickly, so stay by the grill.

Chicken takes readily to the flavors of cuisines around the world, and India's fragrant array of spices are no exception. Here, I have opted to marinate boneless chicken thighs, rather than chicken breasts, in my version of a tandoori marinade for two reasons: the dark meat stands up better to the intense spice mixture, and it doesn't dry out as easily over the direct heat of the grill.

1 To make the tandoori marinade, in a bowl, whisk together the yogurt, lemon juice, ginger, garlic, coriander, turmeric, saffron, cumin, cayenne pepper, 1 teaspoon salt, and ½ teaspoon black pepper.

2 Cut the chicken thighs into 1-inch (2.5-cm) cubes. Place the chicken cubes in a large lock-top plastic bag and pour in the marinade. Seal the bag closed, squish the marinade around the chicken, and refrigerate overnight.

3 At least 30 minutes before you are ready to begin grilling, remove the chicken from the refrigerator. Discard the marinade. If using wooden skewers, soak them in water for 30 minutes.

4 Prepare a charcoal or gas grill for direct grilling over high heat (page 16 or 18). Brush and oil the grill grate.

5 Thread the chicken cubes onto the skewers without crowding them. Place the skewers on the grill directly over the fire and cook, turning once, until the chicken is lightly grill-marked on both sides and opaque throughout but still moist, about 5 minutes on each side. If the chicken begins to burn, move the skewers to the edge of a charcoal grill or lower the heat of a gas grill.

6 Slide the chicken off the skewers onto a platter. Top with the onion and cilantro and serve at once.

GOES GREAT WITH Smoky Grilled Potatoes (page 176); Garlic Bread (page 207); Spicy Tomato Jam (page 215)

Pesto Chicken Sandwiches

4 boneless, skinless chicken
breast halves, about 6 oz
(185 g) each

Kosher salt and freshly
ground pepper

1 teaspoon Italian seasoning

Olive oil for brushing

8 slices fontina cheese

8 slices sourdough bread

Mayonnaise (optional)

8 thick tomato slices

4 tablespoons (2 fl oz/60 ml)
pesto, homemade (page 213)
or store-bought

SERVES 4

The Game Plan

- Make pesto; refrigerate
- Season chicken and
  brush with oil
- Set up grill for direct grilling
  over high heat
- Slice cheese and tomato
- Grilling time: 10–16 minutes
- Assemble sandwiches
- DON'T FORGET Use a sturdy
  bread like sourdough, and
  toast the slices on the grill
  for extra flavor.

Here's a recipe that makes perfect use of boneless, skinless
chicken breasts. Serve these flavorful, melted cheese sandwiches
in midsummer when tomatoes are sweet and fresh basil is
abundant. Just be careful not to overcook the chicken, and
you will have a tasty and juicy alternative to a burger.

1 Season the chicken breast halves with salt and pepper and sprinkle evenly
with the Italian seasoning. Brush lightly on all sides with the oil.

2 Prepare a charcoal or gas grill for direct grilling over high heat (page 16
or 18). Brush and oil the grill grate.

3 Place the chicken on the grill directly over the fire and cook until nicely
grill-marked and relatively firm to the touch, 5–8 minutes on each side
depending on the thickness. You want the chicken to be opaque throughout
but still moist and juicy inside. About 2 minutes before the chicken is ready,
place 2 slices of the cheese on each breast half, cover the grill, and allow
the cheese to melt. Put the bread slices along the edge of the grill at the same
time, and turn once after 1 minute to toast both sides.

4 Transfer the chicken and bread slices to a cutting board. Spread the bread
slices with mayonnaise, if desired. Cut each breast half against the grain on
the diagonal into 3–4 pieces. Arrange 1 sliced breast half on each of 4 bread
slices. Top with 2 tomato slices, and then top the tomatoes with 1 tablespoon
of the pesto, spreading it evenly over the tomatoes. Close the sandwiches
with the remaining bread slices, and serve.

GOES GREAT WITH Grilled Panzanella Salad (page 188); Potato Salad
(page 195); Iceburg Wedge with Blue Cheese (page 204)

Chicken Satay
with Spicy Peanut Sauce

FOR THE MARINADE

1 cup (8 fl oz/250 ml) coconut milk

¼ cup (2 fl oz/60 ml) Asian fish sauce

4 cloves garlic, finely chopped

¼ cup (⅓ oz/10 g) chopped fresh cilantro

1 teaspoon curry powder

Freshly ground pepper

4 lb (2 kg) boneless, skinless chicken breasts

16–20 wooden skewers

Spicy Peanut Sauce (page 217) for serving

SERVES 6 AS A MAIN DISH OR 8–10 AS AN APPETIZER

The Game Plan

- Make marinade
- Pound chicken; cut into strips; marinate for 4–8 hours
- Make peanut sauce
- Remove chicken from fridge; discard marinade; pat dry
- Soak skewers in water
- Set up grill for direct grilling over high heat
- Thread chicken onto skewers
- Grilling time: 8 minutes
- DON'T FORGET Pounding the chicken is key—the meat will be more flavorful and cook more evenly.

This take on one of the most popular appetizers in Southeast Asian restaurants is easy to make and everybody seems to like it. The marinade has a hint of curry, which brightens over the hot fire of the grill. If you're pressed for time, you can skip the peanut sauce and the chicken will still taste wonderful.

1 To make the marinade, in a bowl, stir together the coconut milk, fish sauce, garlic, cilantro, curry powder, and 1 teaspoon pepper. Set aside.

2 One at a time, place the chicken breasts between two sheets of plastic wrap, and pound with a meat pounder or rolling pin to an even thickness of about ½ inch (12 mm). Then, using a sharp knife, cut each breast lengthwise into 3 or 4 strips. Throw all the strips into a large lock-top plastic bag and pour in the marinade. Seal the bag closed, squish the marinade around the chicken, and refrigerate for at least 4 hours or up to 8 hours.

3 At least 30 minutes before you are ready to begin grilling, remove the chicken from the refrigerator. Discard the marinade and pat the chicken strips dry with paper towels. Soak the skewers in water for 30 minutes.

4 Prepare a charcoal or gas grill for direct grilling over high heat (page 16 or 18). Brush and oil the grill grate.

5 Thread the chicken strips lengthwise onto the skewers. Place on the grill and cook, turning once, until the chicken is lightly grill-marked on both sides and opaque throughout but still moist, 4 minutes on each side.

6 Arrange the skewers on a platter and let rest for about 5 minutes before serving. Pass the peanut sauce at the table.

GOES GREAT WITH Coconut Rice (page 196); Balsamic Onion and Green Bean Salad (page 200); Cucumber Salad (page 203)

How to grill the perfect
Whole Chicken

Sitting down to a whole roasted chicken is popular nowadays. Indeed, there is hardly a supermarket in the country that doesn't sell rotisserie-roasted chickens. But cooking a bird at home is simple and less expensive, plus you get a flavor bonus when you cook it on a grill.

BUY A GOOD-QUALITY BIRD Buy a chicken, preferably free range or organic, that weighs at least 4 pounds (2 kg) but is not much bigger than 5 pounds (2.5 kg).

SEASON AND TRUSS THE CHICKEN Remove the giblets and neck from the cavity, and pat the chicken dry with paper towels. Liberally season inside and out with salt and pepper, add other seasoning to the cavity—usually herb sprigs—and tie the legs together with kitchen string. The trussing helps the bird to cook more evenly.

PLAN FOR A CRISP SKIN If you have time, season and truss the bird, then wrap loosely in damp paper towels and refrigerate overnight. This will dry the chicken out a bit, which contributes to a crisp skin.

GO THE INDIRECT ROUTE Indirect heat is the only way to go, whether the bird is on the grate or on a spit.

BASTE WITH AN HERB "MOP" Baste the chicken every 15 minutes or so to add bodacious flavor and to keep the chicken moist. For crisp skin, stop basting for the last 15 minutes of cooking.

TAKE THE BIRD'S TEMPERATURE After the chicken has been on the grill for an hour, use an instant-read thermometer to check the temperature of a thigh, away from the bone, every 10 to 15 minutes. You want it to register 170°F (77°C).

GIVE IT A REST Let the chicken rest for 10 minutes or so before cutting it into serving pieces.

GOES GREAT WITH We all know that mashed potatoes (page 198) are a natural with roast chicken, but Grilled Panzanella Salad (page 188), Mac and Cheese (page 196), or even Cheesy Cauliflower Gratin (page 199) are also perfect partners.

Grill-Roasted Chicken
with Herb Mop

1 chicken, 4 lb (2 kg), neck
and giblets removed

Kosher salt and freshly
ground black pepper

6 fresh rosemary sprigs,
each 6 inches (15 cm) long

Herb Mop (page 210)

---

1 At least 30 minutes before you are ready to begin grilling, remove the chicken from the refrigerator. Pat the chicken dry with paper towels, then season inside and out with salt and pepper. Slip the rosemary sprigs into the cavity, then tie the legs together with kitchen string. Set aside about ¼ cup (2 fl oz/60 ml) of the herb mop for serving.

2 Prepare a charcoal or gas grill for indirect grilling over medium heat; the temperature inside the grill should be 350°–375°F (180°–190°C). If using charcoal, bank the lit coals on either side of the grill bed, leaving a strip in the center without heat, and place a drip pan in the center (page 16). If using gas, preheat the burners, then turn off 1 or more of the burners to create a cooler zone (page 19). Brush and oil the grill grate.

3 Place the chicken, breast side up, over the indirect-heat area of the grill. Cook, turning and rotating the bird occasionally, and basting the bird about every 15 minutes with the herb mop, until nicely browned all over and an instant-read thermometer inserted into the thickest part of the thigh away from bone registers 170°F (77°C), or the juices run clear when a thigh joint is pierced with a knife tip. This will take 1–1½ hours.

4 Transfer the chicken to a cutting board, tent with aluminum foil, and let rest for 10 minutes. Cut into serving pieces and arrange on a platter. Pour a little of the reserved herb mop over the finished chicken, and pass the rest alongside. Serve at once.

SERVES 4–6

Greek-Style Butterflied Chicken

1 whole chicken, 3–4 lb (1.5–2 kg), neck and giblets removed

Kosher salt and freshly ground pepper

Greek Marinade (page 210)

SERVES 4–6

The Game Plan

- Make marinade
- Butterfly chicken; marinate for 24–48 hours
- Remove chicken from fridge and discard marinade
- Set up grill for indirect grilling over medium heat
- Grilling time: about 30 minutes
- DON'T FORGET Use the indirect area of the grill if the chicken starts to burn (this will increase the total grilling time).

This method of grilling a whole chicken is so foolproof that I don't know why I don't do it more often. It is simple to take out the backbone with kitchen shears and then flatten the bird. You end up with an evenly cooked, gorgeously browned chicken, here infused with the bright flavors of lemon and fresh herbs.

1 Place the chicken, breast side down, on a cutting board. Using kitchen shears or a large knife, cut along one side of the backbone from the tail to the neck. Pull open the bird, then cut down the other side of the backbone to free it. (Discard the backbone or save it for stock.) Turn the chicken breast side up and open it as flat as possible—like a book. Press down firmly on the breast to break the breastbone—you will hear popping noises—and flatten the bird.

2 Season the chicken generously on both sides with salt and pepper. Put the chicken in a large lock-top plastic bag in which it lies flat and pour in the marinade. Seal the bag closed, squish the marinade around the chicken, and refrigerate the bag flat for at least 24 hours, or 48 hours is better. Be sure to turn the bag over several times while the chicken is marinating.

3 At least 30 minutes before you are ready to begin grilling, remove the chicken from the refrigerator. Discard the marinade and pat the chicken dry.

4 Prepare a charcoal or gas grill for indirect grilling over medium heat; the temperature inside the grill should be 350°–375°F (180°–190°C). If using charcoal, bank the lit coals on one side of the grill bed, and place a drip pan in the area without coals (page 16). If using gas, preheat the burners, then turn off 1 or more of the burners to create a cooler zone (page 19). Brush and oil the grill grate.

5 Place the chicken, skin side down, over the direct-heat area of the grill. Cook for 12–15 minutes. Turn and continue cooking until an instant-read thermometer inserted into the thickest part of a thigh away from bone registers 170°F (77°C), or the juices run clear when a thigh joint is pierced with a knife tip, about 15 minutes longer. If the chicken begins to burn, move it to the indirect-heat area of the grill and add a little more time.

6 Transfer the chicken to a cutting board, tent with aluminum foil, and let rest for 10 minutes. Cut into serving pieces and serve at once.

GOES GREAT WITH Pesto Pasta Salad (page 201); Greek Salad (page 205); Garlic Bread (page 207)

Beer-Can Chicken

1 tablespoon sugar

1 teaspoon dry mustard

1 teaspoon onion powder

1 teaspoon smoked paprika

1 teaspoon garlic powder

½ teaspoon ground coriander

½ teaspoon ground cumin

Kosher salt and freshly ground black pepper

1 chicken, 4 lb (2 kg), neck and giblets removed

1 tablespoon canola oil

1 can (16 fl oz/500 ml) of your favorite beer

About ⅓ cup (3 fl oz/80 ml) cider vinegar, in a spray bottle

SERVES 4–6

The Game Plan

- Make spice mixture
- Coat bird with oil and spices
- Set up grill for indirect grilling over medium heat
- Place bird on beer can
- Grilling time: about 1½ hours
- Spray bird with vinegar every 15 minutes during grilling
- DON'T FORGET Make sure the bird is placed securely on the can so it doesn't tip over, and be careful when removing it from the grill.

My friend Jane Kurtz shared this recipe with me several years ago. The spice blend is perkier than most blends for beer-can chicken. Jane also taught me to spray the chicken while it's cooking with cider vinegar, which keeps it moist and adds a nice hint of acidity. Plus, it is hard to say no to a recipe that directs you to drink half a beer before you start cooking.

1 In a small container with a tight-fitting lid, combine the sugar, mustard, onion powder, paprika, garlic powder, coriander, cumin, 1 teaspoon salt, and ½ teaspoon pepper. Cover tightly and shake vigorously to mix.

2 At least 30 minutes before you are ready to begin grilling, remove the chicken from the refrigerator. Brush the oil evenly all over the surface of the chicken, then season the chicken inside and out with the spice mixture.

3 Prepare a charcoal or gas grill for indirect grilling over medium heat; the temperature inside the grill should be 350°–375°F (180°–190°C). If using charcoal, bank the lit coals on either side of the grill bed, leaving a strip in the center without heat, and place a drip pan in the center (page 16). If using gas, preheat the burners, then turn off 1 or more of the burners to create a cooler zone (page 19). Brush and oil the grill grate.

4 When the grill is ready, open the beer and drink half of it. Set the half-full can on your countertop, and slide the chicken over the top of the can. The base of the can and the ends of the bird's legs should be even. Place the chicken, keeping the can upright, on the grill over the indirect-heat area. The legs will need to touch the grill grate for extra stability. (Beer-can chicken racks are available, and they are worth the investment for the security they bring to this method.) Cook the bird for about 15 minutes, then spray the bird down with vinegar. Continue cooking, spraying the bird every 15 minutes, until an instant-read thermometer inserted into the thickest part of a thigh away from bone registers 170°F (77°C), or the juices run clear when a thigh joint is pierced with a knife tip, about 1½ hours total.

5 Transfer the chicken to a cutting board, taking care with the can of beer, which will be very hot. Let the chicken rest upright, still on the can, for about 10 minutes. Slide the chicken off the can and cut into serving pieces. Serve at once. You could add your favorite sauce, but I don't think you will need it.

GOES GREAT WITH Mac and Cheese (page 196); Vinegar-Braised Collard Greens (page 199); Buttermilk Biscuits (page 206)

Pulled BBQ Chicken Sandwiches

1 cup (8 fl oz/250 ml) low-sodium chicken broth

4 tablespoons (2 oz/60 g) unsalted butter

½ cup (3 oz/90 g) plus 1 tablespoon All-Purpose BBQ Rub (page 208)

½ teaspoon granulated garlic

2 chickens, 4 lb (2 kg) each, neck and giblets removed

4 tablespoons (2 fl oz/60 ml) olive oil

10–12 hamburger or sandwich buns, split

Classic BBQ Sauce (page 212), or your favorite BBQ sauce, for serving

SERVES 10–12

The Game Plan

- Make BBQ rub and BBQ sauce; refrigerate sauce
- Make flavoring for injector; inject chickens with flavoring
- Coat chickens with oil and season with rub
- Set up grill for indirect grilling over medium heat
- Grilling time: 1–1½ hours
- Shred meat; assemble sandwiches
- DON'T FORGET Rotate the birds on the grill occasionally to ensure even cooking.

Here is a riff on pulled pork that's lower in fat and takes less time to make. The chickens get a fair amount of seasoning through an injection that keeps them moist and tender in the grill. After they are cooked, you just let them cool a bit and then go after them like you would if you were shredding pulled pork.

1 In a saucepan over medium heat, combine the broth, butter, 1 tablespoon of the BBQ rub, and the granulated garlic and heat until the butter melts. Stir to combine and remove from the heat. Let cool to room temperature.

2 At least 30 minutes before you are ready to begin grilling, remove the chickens from the refrigerator. Load a marinade injector with the broth mixture and inject the liquid into each chicken in several places. Rub 2 tablespoons of the oil all over each chicken. Rub the remaining ½ cup BBQ rub all over the 2 chickens, dividing it evenly.

3 Prepare a charcoal or gas grill for indirect grilling over medium heat; the temperature inside the grill should be 350°–375°F (180°–190°C). If using charcoal, bank the lit coals on either side of the grill bed, leaving a strip in the center without heat, and place a drip pan in the center (page 16). If using gas, preheat the burners, then turn off 1 or more of the burners to create a cooler zone (page 19). Brush and oil the grill grate.

4 Place the chickens, breast side up, on the grill over the indirect-heat area and cook, rotating the birds occasionally, until an instant-read thermometer inserted into the thickest part of a thigh registers 170°F (77°C), or until the juices run clear when a thigh joint is pierced with the tip of a knife. This will take 1–1½ hours.

5 Transfer the chickens to a cutting board and let rest for 10–15 minutes. When cool enough to handle, remove and discard the skins. Remove the meat from the bones, discarding the bones. Using 2 forks, shred the meat from both chickens.

6 Divide the chicken among the bun bottoms and top with some BBQ sauce. Cap with the bun tops and serve at once.

GOES GREAT WITH Potato Salad (page 195); Creamy Coleslaw (page 202); Chopped Salad (page 204)

Smoked Duck Breasts
with Cherry Compote

¼ cup (2 oz/60 g) kosher salt

2 tablespoons firmly packed
light brown sugar

1 teaspoon *each* chopped fresh
thyme and fresh rosemary

Freshly ground pepper

4 boneless, skin-on duck breast
halves, about 12 oz (375 g) each

FOR THE CHERRY COMPOTE

½ cup (4 fl oz/125 ml)
white wine

¼ cup (2 oz/60 g) sugar

1 lb (500 g) fresh cherries, pitted

¼ cup (2½ oz/75 g) red
currant jelly

1 tablespoon red wine vinegar

1 teaspoon chopped
fresh thyme

About 2 cups applewood or
cherrywood chips, soaked
in water for 30 minutes

SERVES 4

The Game Plan

- Make spice rub; season
  duck; refrigerate overnight

- Make cherry compote

- Soak wood chips; set
  up grill for smoking over
  high heat

- Grilling time: about
  25 minutes

- DON'T FORGET Sear the duck
  at the end for extra-crisp skin.

Rich duck and tart-sweet fruit are always a great match. Here,
I've added one other element: smoke. Duck takes to this method
beautifully because the thick layer of fat under the skin ensures
the meat remains moist.

1 In a small bowl, stir together the salt, sugar, thyme, rosemary, and
1 teaspoon pepper. Sprinkle the mixture over both sides of the duck breast
halves and rub in gently. Place a rack on a rimmed baking sheet, put the
duck breasts on the rack, cover with plastic wrap, and refrigerate overnight.

2 To make the compote, in a small saucepan over medium heat, combine
the wine and sugar and bring to a simmer, stirring until the sugar dissolves.
Add the cherries and cook, stirring occasionally, until the cherries soften and
begin to lose their shape, about 4 minutes. Stir in the currant jelly, vinegar,
and thyme. Remove from the heat. Let cool to room temperature. The compote
will thicken as it cools. (The compote can be made up to 1 week in advance
and refrigerated. Bring to room temperature before serving.)

3 At least 30 minutes before you are ready to begin grilling, remove the
duck breast halves from the refrigerator. Pat dry with paper towels.

4 Prepare a charcoal or gas grill for smoking over high heat (page 17
or 19); the temperature inside the grill should be 400°–425°F (200°–220°C).
If using charcoal, bank the lit coals on either side of the grill bed, leaving
a strip in the center without heat. Place a drip pan in the center strip and fill
the pan with water. Add the 2 cups wood chips to the fire just before grilling.
If using gas, fill the smoker box with up to 2 cups wood chips, then preheat
the grill. Turn off 1 or more of the burners to create a cooler zone. Brush
and oil the grill grate.

5 Place the duck breast halves, skin side down, on the grill over the indirect-
heat area. Cover the grill and cook the duck breasts for about 20 minutes.
Move the breasts to the direct-heat area and cook for about 5 minutes longer
to crisp the skin. The breasts should be medium-rare at this point.

6 Transfer the duck breast halves to a platter and serve hot or at room
temperature. Pass the cherry compote at the table.

GOES GREAT WITH The Best Mashed Potatoes (page 198); Spinach and Bacon
Salad (page 205); Buttery Dinner Rolls (page 207)

Smoked Turkey Breast
South Louisiana Style

1 bone-in, skin-on turkey breast, 5–6 lb (2.5–3 kg)

2 tablespoons canola oil

3–4 tablespoons Creole Spice Rub (page 208)

6–8 cups mixed hickory and applewood chips, soaked in water for 30 minutes

FOR THE CREOLE TOMATO GRAVY

Drippings from pan

¼ cup (1½ oz/45 g) finely chopped shallots

2 cloves garlic, minced

½ cup (4 fl oz/125 ml) tomato sauce

1 tablespoon all-purpose flour

1 cup (8 fl oz/250 ml) low-sodium chicken broth

½ teaspoon dried thyme

Kosher salt and freshly ground pepper

SERVES 6–8

The Game Plan

- Make spice rub; coat turkey with oil and rub

- Soak wood chips; set up grill for smoking over medium-low heat

- Grilling time: 1½–2 hours

- Let turkey rest; make gravy

- DON'T FORGET Give the turkey plenty of time to rest before you carve it.

If a recipe comes from Louisiana—or from anywhere in delta country—you know you're in for a savory treat. Adding smoke to the turkey breast elevates this humble cut of meat to one fine meal. And what's turkey without gravy? The tomato gravy here, a favorite of delta residents, pairs perfectly with the smoky meat.

1 At least 30 minutes before you are ready to begin grilling, remove the turkey from the refrigerator. Brush the entire surface of the turkey breast with the oil, then liberally season the breast on all sides with the spice rub.

2 Prepare a smoker (page 8) or a charcoal or gas grill for smoking over medium-low heat (page 17 or 19); the temperature inside the grill should be 300°–325°F (150°–165°C). If using charcoal, bank the lit coals on either side of the grill bed, leaving a strip in the center without heat, then add about 2 cups of the wood chips to the fire just before grilling. If using gas, fill the smoker box with up to 2 cups of the wood chips, then preheat the grill. Turn off 1 or more of the burners to create a cooler zone. Brush and oil the grill grate.

3 Place a roasting rack in an aluminum roasting pan, and put the turkey breast on the rack. Put the pan over the indirect-heat area of the grill, and pour 1 cup (8 fl oz/250 ml) water into the pan. Cover the grill and smoke the turkey breast until it is a rich golden brown and an instant-read thermometer inserted into the thickest part of the breast away from bone registers 165°F (74°C), 1½–2 hours, adding additional wood chips every 30 minutes or so and more coals as needed if using charcoal.

4 Transfer the turkey to a cutting board, tent with aluminum foil, and let rest. Meanwhile, prepare the gravy: Skim the fat from the drippings in the turkey pan, then measure ½ cup (4 fl oz/125 ml) of the drippings and pour into a sauté pan. Place over low heat, bring to a simmer, and simmer until reduced by about half. Add the shallots and garlic and cook until softened, about 2 minutes. Stir in the tomato sauce and cook for 1 minute. Whisk in the flour and cook, whisking occasionally, for about 2 minutes. Slowly whisk in the broth. Continue to cook, stirring often, until thickened, 2–3 minutes. Stir in the thyme and season with salt and pepper. Pour into a warmed bowl.

5 Slice the turkey, arrange it on a platter, and serve at once with the gravy.

GOES GREAT WITH Mac and Cheese (page 196); Vinegar-Braised Collard Greens (page 199); Skillet Corn Bread (page 206)

How to grill the perfect
Fish Fillets

Most folks like grilled fish fillets but they don't like to do the grilling. They fear the fish will stick to the grate and they won't be able to get it unstuck. So they order grilled fillets in restaurants and let someone else do the cooking. Here is how to get past that fear and start grilling fillets at home.

BUY THE RIGHT FISH The most common mistake people make is buying the wrong kind of fish. Don't reach for flounder, sole, or other thin, delicate flatfish fillets. Go for meaty and/or oily fish, such as tuna, salmon, grouper, mackerel, sea bass, or striped bass.

MEASURE THE FILLETS Ideally, the fish fillets are at least 1 inch (2.5 cm) thick at their thickest point. Thinner fillets can sometimes dry out before they have a chance to pick up that good grill flavor.

BRUSH ON THE MAYO I usually call for oiling the grill grate. The reverse is true with fish fillets. Although it is still a good idea to oil the grate as a precaution, fish fillets cook best when the fillets themselves are lubricated—and mayonnaise is the ideal lubricant. Don't worry if you hate mayonnaise, because you'll never taste it. Brush a fillet on all sides with mayonnaise, and I guarantee it won't stick when you try to turn it.

CLEAN THE GRATE The mayonnaise definitely helps prevent sticking, but the most important factor when grilling fish fillets—or fish steaks or whole fish—is an impeccably clean grill grate. It does not have to be as shiny as the day it was bought, but all the carbonized proteins should be removed.

GOES GREAT WITH A pat of flavored butter, like the one used here, is a great way to finish off grilled fish. Serve it with Potato Salad (page 195) or a big green salad—I like the Spinach and Bacon Salad (page 205)—for an awesome summertime feast.

Grilled Salmon Fillets
with Herb Butter

FOR THE HERB BUTTER

1 tablespoon *each* finely chopped fresh chives, fresh dill, and fresh tarragon

Kosher salt and freshly ground pepper

½ cup (4 oz/125 g) unsalted butter, at room temperature

¼ lemon

6 skin-on center-cut salmon fillets, each about 8 oz (250 g) and 1 inch (2.5 cm) thick, pin bones removed

¼ cup (2 fl oz/60 ml) mayonnaise, homemade (page 216) or store-bought

2 teaspoons *each* ground cumin and ground coriander

Kosher salt and freshly ground pepper

---

1 To make the butter, in a small bowl, using a fork, work the chives, dill, tarragon, a pinch of salt, and a few grinds of pepper into the butter, distributing the herbs evenly. Squeeze the juice from the lemon into the butter and work it in. Using a spatula, scrape the butter out of the bowl into a rough log shape near one long edge of a 12-by-6-inch (30-by-15-cm) sheet of waxed paper. Roll the paper over the butter, and press the butter into a solid, uniform log. Continue rolling the waxed paper around the butter, and twist both ends to seal securely. Refrigerate to harden. (The butter can be made up to 5 days in advance and refrigerated or frozen for up to 1 month.)

2 Prepare a charcoal or gas grill for direct grilling over high heat (page 16 or 18). Brush and oil the grill grate.

3 Brush the salmon fillets on all sides with the mayonnaise, coating evenly. Sprinkle the cumin and then the coriander evenly over each fillet, then sprinkle salt and pepper evenly over the fillets.

4 Place the salmon fillets, skin side up, on the grill directly over the fire and cook for about 3 minutes. Turn and cook until the fish flakes when prodded gently with a fork, about 3 minutes longer. The salmon will be cooked to medium, which is perfect for salmon.

5 Transfer the fillets to individual plates and top each fillet with a pat of the butter. Serve at once.

SERVES 6

Spiced Mahimahi
with Grilled Pineapple Salsa

Grilled Pineapple Salsa
(page 215) for serving

4 mahimahi fillets, each
about 8 oz (250 g) and
½ inch (12 mm) thick

2 tablespoons mayonnaise

1 tablespoon Latin Spice Rub
(page 208)

SERVES 4

The Game Plan

- Set up grill for direct grilling over high heat
- Make pineapple salsa
- Make spice rub
- Coat fish with mayo and season with rub
- Grilling time: 4–8 minutes
- DON'T FORGET Let the fillets cook, undisturbed, for a couple of minutes before you try to flip them.

Mahimahi, aka dolphin fish, has a stronger flavor than most white fish, and that extra flavor is what makes it a perfect candidate for the grill. Match it up with a little Latin spice and a minty pineapple salsa, and you are sitting down to a wonderful summer supper.

1 Prepare a charcoal or gas grill for direct grilling over high heat (page 16 or 18). Brush and oil the grill grate.

2 Make the pineapple salsa and set aside. (Or, make the salsa up to 2 days in advance and refrigerate until ready to use.)

3 Brush the fillets on both sides with the mayonnaise, coating evenly. Then sprinkle the fillets evenly on both sides with the rub.

4 Place the fish on the grill directly over the fire and cook, turning once, until it is just opaque throughout and flakes when prodded gently with a fork. For the timing, follow the rule of about 8 minutes total per inch (2.5 cm) of thickness. Most mahimahi fillets are about ½ inch (12 mm) thick, so the fish should be done in 4–6 minutes. If your fillets are thicker, cook them just a few minutes longer.

5 Transfer to a platter or individual plates and serve at once. Pass the pineapple salsa at the table.

GOES GREAT WITH Grilled Corn with Lime Butter (page 165); Mexican Rice (page 197); Garlic Bread (page 207)

Grilled Fish Tacos
with Creamy Avocado Salsa

FOR THE TEQUILA MARINADE

Grated zest of 1 lime

2 tablespoons fresh lime juice

2 tablespoons tequila

2 tablespoons fresh
orange juice

1 teaspoon agave nectar
or honey

2 lb (1 kg) skinless mahimahi,
grouper, halibut, snapper, or
other firm white fish fillets

¼ cup (2 fl oz/60 ml)
mayonnaise, homemade
(page 216) or store-bought

24 corn tortillas, about 6 inches
(15 cm) in diameter

2 cups (6 oz/185 g) finely
shredded green cabbage

Creamy Avocado Salsa
(page 215) for serving

½ cup (¾ oz/20 g) coarsely
chopped fresh cilantro

SERVES 4–6

The Game Plan

- Make marinade; marinate
  fish for 30 minutes

- Make salsa; refrigerate

- Set up grill for direct grilling
  over high heat

- Grilling time: about 8 minutes

- Assemble tacos

- DON'T FORGET The grilling
  time will depend on the
  thickness of the fish fillets.

Mahimahi is my first choice for this recipe, but I have suggested other firm white fish that will work well, too. All the fish needs is a quick bath in a little tequila and lime and a few minutes on the grill, and you've got a top-notch filling for tacos. If you can find thick, freshly made tortillas, you only need to use one per taco.

1 To make the tequila marinade, in a small bowl, whisk together the lime zest and juice, tequila, orange juice, and agave. Pour into a shallow baking dish large enough to accommodate the fish fillets in a single layer.

2 Add the fish fillets to the marinade, turn to coat, and marinate at room temperature for 15 minutes. Flip the fish and marinate for 15 minutes more.

3 Prepare a charcoal or gas grill for direct grilling over high heat (page 16 or 18). Brush and oil the grill grate.

4 Remove the fish from the marinade and discard the marinade. Brush the fish on both sides with the mayonnaise, coating evenly.

5 Place the fish on the grill directly over the fire and cook, turning once, until it is just opaque throughout and flakes when prodded gently with a fork. For the timing, follow the rule of about 8 minutes total per inch (2.5 cm) of thickness. Transfer the fish to a platter. Warm the tortillas on the grill, about 1 minute on each side, then stack and wrap in a kitchen towel.

6 Using a fork, break up the fish into bite-sized chunks. To assemble each taco, overlap 2 tortillas, top with some of the fish, a little of the cabbage, a generous spoonful of the salsa, and a sprinkle of the cilantro. Serve at once.

GOES GREAT WITH Drunken Pinto Beans (page 194); Grilled Veggies (page 201); Creamy Coleslaw (page 202)

Moroccan-Style Halibut

6 halibut fillets, each about 8 oz
(250 g) and 1 inch (2.5 cm) thick

2 tablespoons mayonnaise

2 teaspoons ground cumin

1 teaspoon ground coriander

½ teaspoon ground cinnamon

½ teaspoon cayenne pepper

Kosher salt and freshly ground
black pepper

¼ cup (2½ oz/75 g)
pomegranate molasses,
warmed

Chopped fresh cilantro
for serving

6 lime wedges

SERVES 6

The Game Plan

- Set up grill for direct grilling
  over high heat

- Brush fish with mayo and
  season with spices

- Grilling time: about 8 minutes

- Brush fish with warm molasses
  after grilling

- DON'T FORGET Make sure
  your grill grates are very
  clean and well oiled before
  grilling the fish.

Halibut is a thick, meaty fish that has great texture and readily absorbs the flavors of all kinds of seasonings. Here, I treat it to a quartet of spices to give it a North African accent before it goes over the fire, and then top off the grilled fillets with a glaze of sweet, bitter, tart pomegranate molasses.

1 Prepare a charcoal or gas grill for direct grilling over high heat (page 16 or 18). Brush and oil the grill grate.

2 Brush the fish on both sides with the mayonnaise, coating evenly. In a small bowl, stir together the cumin, coriander, cinnamon, and cayenne. Sprinkle the fish evenly on both sides with the spice mixture, then season on both sides with salt and black pepper.

3 Place the fish on the grill directly over the fire and cook, turning once, until it is just opaque throughout and flakes when prodded gently with a fork, about 4 minutes on each side.

4 Transfer the fish to a platter or individual plates. Brush each fillet with a thin coat of the warm pomegranate molasses, sprinkle with cilantro, and serve with the lime wedges.

GOES GREAT WITH Grilled Eggplant with Feta (page 172); Herbed Rice Pilaf (page 197); Watermelon Salad (page 203)

Coconut-Lime Fish Fillets

4 sea bass, red snapper, grouper, or other firm white fish fillets, each about 8 oz (250 g) and 1 inch (2.5 cm) thick

2 tablespoons mayonnaise

Kosher salt and freshly ground pepper

Coconut-Lime Sauce (page 217), warmed, for serving

½ cup (3 oz/90 g) dry-roasted peanuts, chopped

¼ cup (⅓ oz/10 g) chopped fresh cilantro

SERVES 4

The Game Plan

- Make coconut sauce; keep warm

- Set up grill for direct grilling over high heat

- Coat fish with mayo and seasonings

- Grilling time: about 8 minutes

- Pour sauce over fish after grilling

- DON'T FORGET Brushing a thin, even coating of mayonnaise on the fillets will help keep them from sticking to the grill grates.

If you're wishing for a quick trip to the Caribbean, fire up your grill and cook this dish while you indulge in a mojito and listen to some Jimmy Buffet. A lot of sweet and tart is going on here, and almost any white fish that is thick enough for the grill will accept these flavors, so buy whatever is freshest in the market.

1 Prepare a charcoal or gas grill for direct grilling over high heat (page 16 or 18). Brush and oil the grill grate.

2 Brush the fish fillets on both sides with the mayonnaise, coating evenly. Season with salt and pepper.

3 Place the fish on the grill and cook, turning once, until it is just opaque throughout and flakes when prodded gently with a fork. For the timing, follow the rule of about 8 minutes total per inch (2.5 cm) of thickness.

4 Transfer the fillets to a platter. Ladle some of the warm coconut-lime sauce over each fillet, sprinkle with the peanuts and cilantro, and serve at once. Pass the remaining sauce at the table.

GOES GREAT WITH Grilled Corn with Lime Butter (page 165); Coconut Rice (page 196); Cucumber Salad (page 203)

Smoked Salmon
with Lemon-Garlic Aioli

¼ cup (2 oz/60 g) firmly packed light brown sugar

¼ cup (2 oz/60 g) kosher salt

1 tablespoon chopped fresh dill

4 skin-on center-cut salmon fillets, each about 8 oz (250 g) and 1 inch (2.5 cm) thick, pin bones removed

FOR THE LEMON-GARLIC AIOLI

3–4 cloves garlic, unpeeled

2 large egg yolks, fresh or pasteurized

Grated zest of 1 lemon

2 tablespoons fresh lemon juice, or to taste

Kosher salt

½ cup (4 fl oz/125 ml) canola oil or ¼ cup (2 fl oz/60 ml) *each* canola oil and olive oil

About 2 cups applewood chips, soaked in water for 30 minutes

SERVES 4

The Game Plan

- Season fillets; refrigerate for 2–4 hours
- Make aioli; refrigerate
- Soak wood chips; set up grill for smoking over medium heat
- Rinse salmon and pat dry
- Grilling time: 15–20 minutes
- DON'T FORGET Cover the grill to infuse the salmon with smoky flavor.

Preparing hot-smoked salmon is a piece of cake. You just rub the fillets with a sugar-salt "cure," refrigerate them for a few hours to draw out a little moisture, and then smoke them in a covered grill for no more than 20 minutes. I always smoke extra fillets, which I freeze and then add to salads or mix with cream cheese for a dip.

1 Set a large cooling rack in a rimmed baking sheet. In a small bowl, stir together the sugar, salt, and dill. Lightly rub the mixture on all sides of the fillets, then place the fillets on the rack and cover the whole thing with plastic wrap. Refrigerate for at least 2 hours or up 4 hours.

2 To make the aioli, preheat the oven to 350°F (180°C). Wrap the garlic in aluminum foil, place on a baking sheet, and bake until soft, about 40 minutes. (You can skip this step and substitute 1 tablespoon store-bought puréed roasted garlic.) Let the garlic cool, then squeeze the flesh into a small food processor or a blender. Add the egg yolks and lemon zest and juice and pulse to combine. Sprinkle in a pinch of salt. With the machine running, slowly add the oil in a thin, steady stream and process until the mixture thickens to the consistency of mayonnaise. Taste and adjust the seasoning. If the mixture seems too thick, thin it with a little warm water. Cover and refrigerate until serving. (The aioli can be made up to 3 days in advance and refrigerated.)

3 Prepare a charcoal or gas grill for smoking over medium heat (page 17 or 19); the temperature inside the grill should be 350°–375°F (180°–190°C). If using charcoal, bank the lit coals on either side of the grill bed, leaving a strip in the center without heat. Place a drip pan in the center strip and fill the pan with water. Add the 2 cups wood chips to the fire just before grilling. If using gas, fill the smoker box with up to 2 cups wood chips, then preheat the grill. Turn off 1 or more of the burners to create a cooler zone. Brush and oil the grill grate.

4 Remove the fish fillets from the refrigerator and hold under cold running water to rinse off the cure. Pat dry with paper towels. Place the fillets, skin side down, on the grill over the indirect-heat area. Cover the grill and cook, without turning the fillets, until just opaque throughout, 15–20 minutes.

5 Transfer the salmon to a platter and serve warm or at room temperature. Pass the aioli at the table.

GOES GREAT WITH Smoky Grilled Potatoes (page 176); Greek Salad (page 205); Garlic Bread (page 207)

Plank-Grilled Salmon
with Mustard-Dill Sauce

Beer as needed for soaking (optional)

½ cup (4 oz/125 g) unsalted butter

¼ cup (2 fl oz/60 ml) fresh lemon juice

2 tablospoons chopped fresh flat-leaf parsley

1 teaspoon reduced-sodium soy sauce or tamari

2 lb (1 kg) skin-on center-cut salmon fillet (either 1 large fillet or 4 small fillets), about 1 inch (2.5 cm) thick, pin bones removed

Olive oil for brushing

Sea salt

½ cup (4 oz/125 g) honey mustard

¼ cup (⅓ oz/10 g) chopped fresh dill

SERVES 4

The Game Plan

- Soak plank for at least 1 hour

- Set up grill for direct grilling over high heat

- Make butter mixture

- Oil, season, and heat plank

- Place fish on plank; brush with butter mixture

- Grilling time: 10–12 minutes

- DON'T FORGET Make sure the plank is untreated, and soak it for at least 1 hour.

Grilling salmon on a cedar plank originated with the Native Americans of the Pacific Northwest, and it is now a popular recipe up and down the West Coast. Here, I have paired that tradition with a honey-mustard sauce that is straight out of the Jewish delicatessens of New York. Any leftover salmon will be outstanding on your morning bagel.

1 Soak 1 large or 4 small untreated cedar planks in water or beer to cover for at least 1 hour. (If using the large plank, make sure it is big enough to hold the large fillet. If using small planks, make sure each is large enough to hold 1 small fillet.)

2 Prepare a charcoal or gas grill for direct grilling over high heat (page 16 or 18). Brush and oil the grill grate.

3 In a small saucepan over medium heat, melt the butter. Whisk in the lemon juice, parsley, and soy sauce. Remove from the heat and keep warm.

4 Remove the plank from the water. Brush one side generously with olive oil and sprinkle with the salt. Place the plank on the grill directly over the fire, cover the grill, and heat until it begins to crackle and even smoke a bit, about 5 minutes.

5 Uncover the grill and place the salmon fillet on the plank. Brush the salmon generously with the butter mixture. Re-cover and cook, without turning the fillet, until the fish flakes when prodded gently with a fork, 10–12 minutes. The fillet should be cooked to medium, which is perfect for salmon. Check the plank frequently to make sure it doesn't catch on fire. Have a spray bottle filled with water handy to extinguish any flames (but be careful—the steam created from the water can cause burns).

6 Using heavy-duty pot holders, transfer the plank to a heatproof work surface. Using a spatula, transfer the salmon fillet to a warmed platter. In a small bowl, stir together the mustard and dill. Serve the salmon at once, with the mustard sauce on the side.

GOES GREAT WITH Grilled Asparagus with Lemon Mayonnaise (page 166); Herbed Rice Pilaf (page 197); Chopped Salad (page 204)

Whole Grilled Trout
Stuffed with Lemon and Herbs

About 2 cups applewood chips, soaked in water for 30 minutes

8 fresh thyme sprigs

8 fresh oregano sprigs

4 fresh rosemary sprigs

8 lemon slices, each ¼ inch (6 mm) thick

1 tablespoon chopped garlic

4 small whole trout, about 12 oz (375 g) each, cleaned and heads removed if desired

¼ cup (2 fl oz/60 ml) mayonnaise, homemade (page 216) or store-bought

Extra-virgin olive oil for drizzling

SERVES 4

The Game Plan

- Soak wood chips; set up grill for direct grilling over medium heat

- Stuff trout with herbs, lemon, and garlic

- Secure each cavity; brush fish with mayo

- Grilling time: 10–12 minutes

- DON'T FORGET The trout doesn't take long to cook, so make sure your wood chips are really smoking before you put the trout on the grill.

If you're a fly fisherman, you already know how great wild freshwater trout can be. Farm-raised rainbow trout and golden trout, however, are becoming more widely available and are a good choice when wild-caught fish aren't possible. The key to this dish is the fresh herbs and lemon, which perfume the trout without overpowering its delicate flavor.

1 Prepare a charcoal or gas grill for direct grilling over medium heat (page 16 or 18). If using charcoal, add the 2 cups wood chips to the fire just before grilling (page 17). If using gas, fill the smoker box with up to 2 cups wood chips, then preheat the grill (page 19). Brush and oil the grill grate.

2 Stuff 2 thyme sprigs, 2 oregano sprigs, 1 rosemary sprig, 2 lemon slices, and one-fourth of the garlic in each trout cavity. Use a toothpick to secure each cavity closed, or tie closed with kitchen string. Brush the outside of each trout with the mayonnaise, coating evenly.

3 Wait until you see a good head of smoke rising from the grill. Then place the trout on the grill directly over the fire, cover, and cook, turning once, for 5–6 minutes on each side. Two large spatulas will help you turn them. (The mayonnaise will keep them from sticking to the grill.) The fish is done when you can slide a paring knife into the thickest part of the flesh near the bone, pull it out, and touch it to your lip. If it is warm, you're ready to go.

4 Transfer the trout to individual plates. Drizzle with the oil—make sure it is first rate—and serve at once.

GOES GREAT WITH Herbed Rice Pilaf (page 197); Vinegar-Braised Collard Greens (page 199); Skillet Corn Bread (page 206)

Whole Red Snapper
with Creole Spices and Andouille Sausage

2 whole red snappers, 2½–3 lb (1.25–1.5 kg) each, cleaned with head and tail intact

2–3 tablespoons Creole Spice Rub (page 208)

2 andouille sausages, sliced on the diagonal about ¼ inch (6 mm) thick

4 green onions, including tender green parts, cut into 2-inch (5-cm) pieces

2 tablespoons mayonnaise

SERVES 4

The Game Plan

- Set up grill for indirect grilling over medium heat

- Make spice rub; slice sausages and green onions

- Season and stuff fish

- Secure each cavity; brush fish with mayo

- Grilling time: 15–20 minutes

- DON'T FORGET Whole fish can be a bit unwieldy on the grill—use 2 large spatulas to turn them, or better yet, use a grill basket.

Don't be afraid to grill a whole fish. Just know that when it comes time to turn it, you'll need a nice long spatula or two shorter ones. I stuff the cavity with andouille sausage, which infuses the fish with a smoky, spicy flavor. Don't skimp on the mayonnaise—it keeps the fish from sticking to the grill.

1 Prepare a charcoal or gas grill for indirect grilling over medium heat; the temperature inside the grill should be 350°–375°F (180°–190°C). If using charcoal, bank the lit coals on either side of the grill bed, leaving a strip in the center without heat, and place a drip pan in the center (page 16). If using gas, preheat the burners, then turn off 1 or more of the burners to create a cooler zone (page 19). Brush and oil the grill grate.

2 Season both fish liberally inside and out with the spice rub. Place half of the andouille slices and green onion pieces in each cavity. Use a toothpick to secure each cavity closed, or tie closed with kitchen string. Brush 1 tablespoon of the mayonnaise on both sides of each fish.

3 Place the fish on the grill over the indirect-heat area. Usually you cook a fish for 8–10 minutes per inch (2.5 cm) of thickness. Whole fish take longer, so figure on 15–20 minutes total, turning the fish halfway through. Two large spatulas will help you turn them. The fish is done when you can slide a paring knife into the thickest part of the flesh near the bone, pull it out, and touch it to your lip. If it is warm, you're ready to go. Check the fish often toward the end of the cooking time. Nothing is worse than overcooked fish.

4 Using the spatulas, transfer the fish to a large platter and let rest for about 5 minutes. One at a time, carefully lift the top fillet from each fish, then lift away and discard the central bone. Serve at once. Be sure you don't forget the fish cheeks. They are real treats.

GOES GREAT WITH Southwestern Bean Salad (page 195); Balsamic Onion and Green Bean Salad (page 200); Skillet Corn Bread (page 206)

Spicy Shrimp Kebabs
with Chipotle Sauce

48 large shrimp in the shell, about 2 lb (1 kg) total weight

Basic Shrimp Brine (page 211)

FOR THE CHIPOTLE SAUCE

1 chipotle chile in adobo sauce

½ cup (4 oz/125 g) sour cream

½ cup (4 fl oz/125 g) mayonnaise, preferably homemade (page 216)

1 teaspoon fresh lime juice

2 tablespoons chopped fresh cilantro

Kosher salt and freshly ground pepper

10 wooden skewers (optional)

2 tablespoons canola oil

2–3 tablespoons Cumin Crust Rub (page 208)

¼ teaspoon cayenne pepper

SERVES 4–6

The Game Plan

- Make brine; devein shrimp; brine for 1½ hours
- Make sauce; refrigerate
- Set up grill for direct grilling over high heat
- Make rub; season shrimp
- Grilling time: about 6 minutes
- DON'T FORGET Pull the shrimp off the grill as soon as they turn opaque.

Before you get to work on this dish, read the tips on how to grill perfect shrimp (page 154). After brining, I coat the shrimp in a potent cumin rub that imparts plenty of flavor, and then serve them with a creamy, lightly spiced chipotle sauce that nicely tempers the intensity of both the rub and the smoke.

1 About 2 hours before you are ready to begin grilling, snip open the shell along the length of the back of each shrimp using kitchen scissors. Then, using the tip of a small knife, cut a shallow groove along the length of the vein and lift it out. Add the shrimp to the brine, cover, and refrigerate for about 1½ hours.

2 To make the sauce, finely chop the chipotle chile. In a bowl, whisk together the sour cream, mayonnaise, chile, and lime juice. Stir in the cilantro and season to taste with salt and pepper. Cover and refrigerate until serving. (The sauce can be made up to 4 days in advance.)

3 Prepare a charcoal or gas grill for direct grilling over high heat (page 16 or 18). Brush and oil the grill grate. I like to skewer the shrimp because it makes them easier to turn, but it is not necessary. If you want to skewer, soak wooden skewers in water for at least 30 minutes.

4 Remove the shrimp from the brine and discard the brine. Pat the shrimp dry with paper towels and place in a bowl. Drizzle with the oil and toss to coat evenly. In a small bowl, stir together the cumin rub and cayenne pepper. Sprinkle the mixture over the shrimp and toss to coat evenly. If skewering, hold 2 skewers parallel and about 1 inch (2.5 cm) apart, and skewer the shrimp onto both skewers, once near the tail and once near the head.

5 Place the shrimp on the grill directly over the fire and cook for 3 minutes. Turn and cook until the shrimp turn creamy white, about 3 minutes more. This could happen after only 2 minutes on the second side, so pay attention.

6 Transfer the shrimp to a platter, or slide the shrimp off onto the platter if skewered. Let everyone peel their own shrimp. Serve with the chipotle sauce.

GOES GREAT WITH Grilled Corn with Lime Butter (page 165); Mexican Rice (page 197); Chopped Salad (page 204)

Barbecued Oysters
Western Maryland Style

48 medium-sized oysters

½ cup (4 oz/125 g) unsalted butter

6 cloves garlic, finely chopped

½ cup (4 fl oz/125 ml) Classic BBQ Sauce (page 212) or your favorite BBQ sauce

SERVES 4 AS A MAIN DISH OR 8 AS AN APPETIZER

The Game Plan

• **Make BBQ sauce; refrigerate**

• **Scrub and shuck oysters; refrigerate until ready to grill**

• **Set up grill for direct grilling over high heat**

• **Make butter sauce**

• **Grilling time: about 5 minutes**

• **DON'T FORGET** Once you've shucked the oysters, be careful not to tip them over or their delicious briny juices will spill out.

When Maryland and the Chesapeake Bay are mentioned, most of us automatically think of the Eastern Shore. You might be surprised to discover that some of the best cooking is found on the opposite shore of the bay. These deceptively simple oysters are served at festivals throughout the region during the fall and winter months when oysters are abundant.

1 Scrub the oysters with a stiff brush under cold running water. To shuck each oyster, hold it, flat side up, in your nondominant hand. (You might want to protect your hand from the sharp shell with a folded kitchen towel or a sturdy glove.) Find the hinge near the pointed end of the oyster, and insert the tip of an oyster knife about ½ inch (12 mm) deep into the hinge. Twist the knife to break the hinge and loosen the top shell. Slide the knife along the inside surface of the top shell to detach the muscle that connects it to the oyster, and remove the top shell. Run the knife along the inside surface of the bottom shell to loosen the oyster, and leave the oyster in the shell. Place the oyster on a rimmed baking sheet or tray and repeat with the remaining oysters. Once all the oysters are shucked, return them to the refrigerator until the grill is ready.

2 Prepare a charcoal or gas grill for direct grilling over high heat (page 16 or 18). Brush and oil the grill grate.

3 In a small saucepan over medium heat, melt the butter. Add the garlic and BBQ sauce. Whisk to combine. Simmer for 5 minutes to blend the flavors, then remove from the heat.

4 Carefully place the oysters on the grill and quickly spoon a little of the sauce into each shell. Cover the grill and cook for about 5 minutes, or until the oysters are to your liking.

5 Using tongs, transfer the oysters to a platter and serve at once.

GOES GREAT WITH Grilled Corn with Lime Butter (page 165); Spinach and Bacon Salad (page 205); Garlic Bread (page 207)

How to grill the perfect
Shrimp

Cooking shrimp on the grill seems to frustrate people more than grilling any other seafood. And that's a shame because shrimp pick up a particularly wonderful flavor cooked over fire. The main problem is timing: if you cook shrimp even 10 seconds too long, you end up with rubber instead of great taste. Here is some advice to help the frustrated shrimp griller.

BUY LARGE SHRIMP By that I mean you want your shrimp to weigh in at 24 per pound (500 g). The larger the shrimp, the longer they can stay on the grill and develop that deep, smoky flavor that you're going for.

KEEP THE SHELL ON The shell traps the shrimp flavor that we all crave, and also helps protect the tender meat. So grill them with the shell on, and let folks shell their own shrimp at the table.

REMOVE THE VEIN If you don't like the look of the dark vein, you can get rid of it: Use kitchen scissors to snip open the shell along the length of the back of the shrimp. Using the tip of a small knife, cut a shallow groove along the length of the vein and lift it out. You have not only gotten rid of the vein, but you will also be able to see a little deeper into the shrimp to know when it is done.

BRINE YOUR SHRIMP Brining gives you just enough fudge factor to get away with a little overcooking, should you turn away from the grill at a critical point. Be careful that you don't brine the shrimp for longer than 1½ hours, or else the brine could break down the muscles too much and result in mushy shrimp (yuck).

GOES GREAT WITH Serve these shrimp with a tangy cocktail sauce for the perfect appetizer to distract people while you grill the main course. You can also grill some chicken wings along with the shrimp—Spicy Buffalo Wings (page 109) or Honey-Sesame Wings (page 112) are both great.

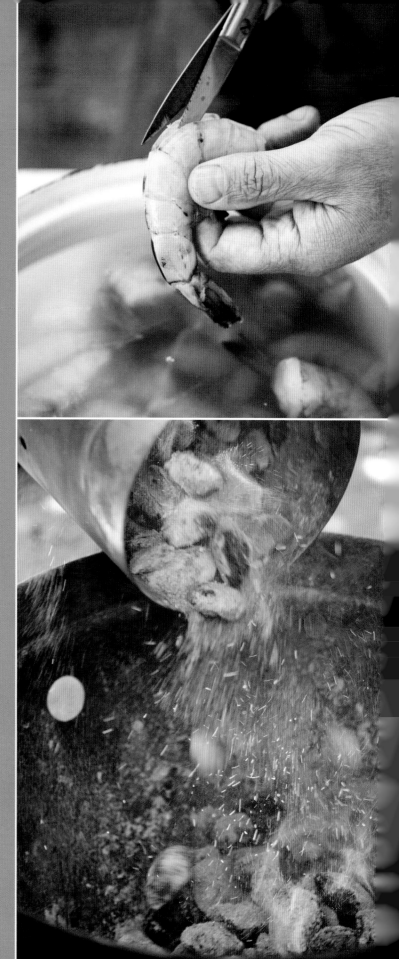

Grilled Shrimp Cocktail

FOR THE COCKTAIL SAUCE

1 cup (8 oz/250 g) ketchup

1 tablespoon grated fresh
or jarred horseradish

1 teaspoon Worcestershire sauce

1 teaspoon sugar

Squeeze of fresh lemon juice

10 wooden skewers (optional)

48 large shrimp in the shell,
about 2 lb (1 kg) total weight

Basic Shrimp Brine (page 211)

2 tablespoons canola oil

---

1 To make the cocktail sauce, in a small bowl, whisk together the ketchup, horseradish, Worcestershire, sugar, and lemon juice. Set aside at room temperature. I like to skewer the shrimp because it makes them easier to turn, but it is not necessary. If you want to skewer, soak the wooden skewers in water for at least 30 minutes.

2 About 2 hours before you are ready to begin grilling, snip open the shell along the length of the back of each shrimp using kitchen scissors. Then, using the tip of a small knife, cut a shallow groove along the length of the vein and lift it out. Add the shrimp to the brine, cover, and refrigerate for 1½ hours.

3 Prepare a charcoal or gas grill for direct grilling over high heat (page 16 or 18). Brush and oil the grill grate.

4 Remove the shrimp from the brine and discard the brine. Pat the shrimp dry with paper towels and place in a bowl. Drizzle with the oil and toss to coat evenly. If skewering, hold 2 skewers parallel and about 1 inch (2.5 cm) apart, and skewer the shrimp onto both skewers, once near the tail end and once near the head. You should be able to get 5 or 6 shrimp on a pair of 10-inch (25-cm) skewers.

5 Place the shrimp on the grill directly over the fire and cook for 3 minutes. Turn and cook until the shrimp turn creamy white, about 3 minutes more. This could happen after only 2 minutes on the second side, so pay attention.

6 Transfer the shrimp to a platter. If you have used skewers, slide the shrimp off onto the platter. Let everybody peel their own shrimp. Enjoy with the cocktail sauce.

SERVES 6–8 AS AN APPETIZER

Cajun Shrimp and Sausage Skewers

6–12 metal or wooden skewers

6 small red-skinned
potatoes, halved

2 ears corn, shucked and cut
into rings 1 inch (2.5 cm) thick

24 large shrimp in the shell,
about 1 lb (500 g) total weight

1 lb (500 g) andouille sausages,
thickly sliced crosswise

2 tablespoons Cajun Seasoning
(page 209)

SERVES 6–8

The Game Plan

- Soak skewers if using wooden

- Prepare potatoes and corn;
  boil for 5 minutes

- Make seasoning;
  devein shrimp

- Thread ingredients
  onto skewers; season

- Set up grill for direct grilling
  over medium heat

- Grilling time: 6–10 minutes

- DON'T FORGET It's important
  to precook the potatoes
  and corn so they'll be done
  at the same time as the
  sausages and shrimp.

A favorite pastime in southern Louisiana is to invite everyone over for a big shrimp boil. These skewers—packed with shrimp and heady with andouille sausage, corn, and potatoes—give you the same flavors but with a lot less work. Plus, the grill adds some of its own smoky, charred flavor to the mix.

1 If using wooden skewers, soak them in water for at least 30 minutes.

2 Bring a large saucepan three-fourths full of water to a boil over high heat. Drop the potatoes and corn into the boiling water and cook for 5 minutes. Drain and immerse in ice water to halt the cooking.

3 Using kitchen scissors, snip open the shell along the length of the back of each shrimp. Then, using the tip of a small knife, cut a shallow groove along the length of the vein and lift it out. Thread the shrimp, sausages, and vegetables onto each skewer, dividing them evenly. Place the skewers on a tray or platter, and sprinkle them evenly with the cajun seasoning. Let them sit while you ready the fire.

4 Prepare a charcoal or gas grill for direct grilling over medium heat (page 16 or 18). Brush and oil the grill grate.

5 Place the skewers on the grill directly over the fire. Cook, turning once (tongs are handy for turning the skewers), until the shrimp turn creamy white and the potatoes are tender, 3–5 minutes on each side.

6 Slide the shrimp, sausages, and vegetables off the skewers onto a platter and serve at once.

GOES GREAT WITH Mac and Cheese (page 196); Vinegar-Braised Collard Greens (page 199); Skillet Corn Bread (page 206)

Lobster Tails
with Zesty Butter

½ cup (4 oz/125 g)
unsalted butter

2 cloves garlic, finely chopped

1 tablespoon finely
chopped shallot

1 tablespoon chopped fresh
tarragon (optional)

Finely grated zest of 1 lemon

Kosher salt

8 metal or wooden skewers

8 lobster tails, about
¼ lb (125 g) each

Lemon wedges for serving

SERVES 4

The Game Plan

- Make flavored butter;
  soak skewers

- Set up grill for direct grilling
  over high heat

- Prepare lobsters for grilling

- Grilling time: 7–8 minutes

- Add flavored butter during
  and after grilling

- DON'T FORGET Skewer the
  lobster tails so they stay flat
  on the grill and don't curl.

If you want to impress your guests, grilled lobster tails are an excellent choice. Here, I have dressed them up by taking the flavors of a classic béarnaise sauce and infusing them into a compound butter, which I add to the lobster both on the grill and just before serving. The rich, decadent result will bring a round of applause at your table.

1 In a small saucepan over low heat, melt the butter. Stir in the garlic, shallot, tarragon, if using, and lemon zest. Remove from the heat, season with salt, and set aside. If using wooden skewers, soak them in water for at least 30 minutes.

2 Prepare a charcoal or gas grill for direct grilling over high heat (page 16 or 18). Brush and oil the grill grate.

3 Cut away the thin undershell from each lobster tail, leaving the hard outer shell. Run a skewer down the length of each lobster tail. This will help to keep the tails flat on the grill. Place the tails, meat side down, on the grill and cook for about 3 minutes. Turn the lobster tails over and spoon about half of the butter over the meat of each tail. Cook just until the meat turns creamy white, 4–5 minutes more.

4 Transfer the lobster tails to a platter and slide them off the skewers. Spoon more of the butter over each tail. Serve at once with the lemon wedges.

GOES GREAT WITH Grilled Asparagus with Lemon Mayonnaise (page 166); Grilled Veggies (page 201); Garlic Bread (page 207)

Bacon-Wrapped Prawns

24 large shrimp in the shell, about 1 lb (500 g) total weight, peeled with tail segment intact

Basic Shrimp Brine (page 211)

6–8 metal or wooden skewers

12 slices thick-cut applewood-smoked bacon, cut in half

24 large fresh basil leaves

SERVES 4–6

The Game Plan

- Make brine; devein shrimp; brine shrimp for 30 minutes

- Soak skewers in water if using wooden

- Set up grill for direct grilling over high heat

- Poach bacon for 5 minutes

- Remove shrimp from brine and discard brine; pat dry

- Wrap basil and bacon around shrimp; skewer

- Grilling time: 6–10 minutes

- DON'T FORGET Check the shrimp often to make sure they don't overcook.

This is a riff on a recipe I learned from the King of Country Hams, Allen Benton, of Madisonville, Tennessee. One trick I use here is poaching the bacon before I wrap it around the shrimp, which guarantees crispy bacon when the shrimp are done. (I do the same thing in the recipe for filets mignons on page 48.) Benton uses prosciutto, which ain't bad, either.

1 Using the tip of a small knife, cut a shallow groove along the back of each shrimp, exposing the dark vein. Lift out the vein with the knife tip. Add the shrimp to the brine, cover, and refrigerate for 30 minutes.

2 Prepare a charcoal or gas grill for direct grilling over high heat (page 16 or 18). Brush and oil the grill grate. If using wooden skewers, soak them in water for at least 30 minutes.

3 Bring a saucepan three-fourths full of water to a boil over high heat. Drop in the bacon slices, reduce the heat to medium, and simmer for 5 minutes. Drain and dry on paper towels.

4 Remove the shrimp from the brine and discard the brine. Pat the shrimp dry with paper towels. Wrap 1 basil leaf tightly around the middle of each shrimp, and then wrap a half slice of bacon around the basil. Slide the wrapped shrimp onto a skewer, piercing it through the middle and securing the bacon and basil. Repeat with the remaining shrimp, bacon, and basil.

5 Place the shrimp on the grill and cook, turning once, until the bacon is a little crispy and the shrimp turn creamy white, 3–5 minutes on each side.

6 Slide the shrimp off the skewers onto a platter. Serve at once.

GOES GREAT WITH Bruschetta with Three Toppings (page 191); Pesto Pasta Salad (page 201); Iceberg Wedge with Blue Cheese (page 204)

OTHER STUFF

How to grill the perfect
Corn on the Cob

I probably know of twenty different methods for grilling corn on the cob. Some folks like to leave it in the husk, soak it in water, and grill it that way. Others will open the husk up, remove the silk, put in a flavored butter, tie it back up, and then grill. And still others will completely shuck the corn, wrap it in aluminum foil, and put it on the grill. To me, all these methods are too much trouble.

SHUCK THE CORN Grilled corn on the cob in its husk looks great in a photograph, but it can be a pain to deal with. Also, when grilling corn in the husk or in aluminum foil, you miss out on what happens when the natural sugars in the corn sizzle and marry with the direct heat of the grill, creating a pretty caramelization that boosts the flavor of the corn tenfold.

PAY ATTENTION Grilling corn on the cob is a matter of timing and turning. You really don't want to leave the corn sitting on the grill for very long, especially when it's shucked and doesn't have the husk to protect it. Grill the corn cobs over medium heat for only 5–8 minutes total.

FRESH IS BEST The fresher the corn, the less time it needs to stay on the grill. All those lovely natural sugars will quickly turn to starch, so corn that's been sitting around for awhile will be less sweet and juicy.

TOP IT OFF I like to gild this corn-on-the-cob lily with a fancy butter, and the lime butter here is one of my favorites. It showcases the wonderfully sweet, nutty, creamy flavor of one of summer's best gifts: corn on the cob. But you can also create great butters with smoked paprika, dried thyme and oregano, or even with one of the protein rubs in this book, such as the Latin Spice Rub (page 208) or Creole Spice Rub (page 208). Just mix some to taste into room-temperature butter and you've got a fancy butter.

Grilled Corn
with Lime Butter

FOR THE LIME BUTTER

Finely grated zest of 1 lime

⅛ teaspoon hot-pepper sauce

⅛ teaspoon tequila (optional)

Kosher salt and freshly ground pepper

½ cup (4 oz/125 g) unsalted butter,
at room temperature

4 ears freshly picked corn, preferably
yellow or a yellow and white mix,
shucked and silk removed

---

1 To make the butter, in a small
bowl, using a fork, work the lime zest,
pepper sauce, tequila, a pinch of salt,
and a few grinds of pepper into the
butter, distributing the flavors evenly.
Transfer to an airtight container and
refrigerate until hardened before using.
(You will have enough butter for at least
8 ears of grilled corn. It will keep in
the refrigerator for up to 1 week or
in the freezer for up to 1 month.)

2 Prepare a charcoal or gas grill for
direct grilling over medium heat (page
16 or 18). Brush and oil the grill grate.

3 Place the corn on the grill directly over
the fire and cook, turning every couple of
minutes, all the way around each ear. The
kernels should become bright yellow and
pick up some charring from the grill. You
don't want blackened corn; you just want
an accent of caramelization from the hot
fire. Usually corn needs no more than
5 minutes, or 8 minutes at the most.

4 Transfer the corn to a platter,
slather it with the butter, and serve.

SERVES 4

Grilled Asparagus
with Lemon Mayonnaise

1 lb (500 g) medium-thick asparagus

Olive oil for drizzling

½ cup (4 fl oz/125 ml) mayonnaise, preferably homemade (page 216)

Finely grated zest of 1 lemon

Pinch of kosher salt

SERVES 4

The Game Plan

- Set up grill for direct grilling over medium heat
- Prepare asparagus
- Make lemon mayo
- Grilling time: about 5 minutes
- DON'T FORGET The spears can easily fall through the grill grate, so be careful when turning them, or use a grill basket.

Asparagus is a harbinger of spring. And when the spears are freshly harvested and just a little stouter than pencil thin, they beg to be cooked on the grill. Set out a bowl of tangy lemon mayo, and your guests may forget about the rest of the menu.

1 Prepare a charcoal or gas grill for direct grilling over medium heat (page 16 or 18). Brush and oil the grill grate.

2 Snap or trim off the tough ends of the asparagus spears. Place the asparagus in a shallow baking dish or deep platter, drizzle with the oil, and toss to coat evenly.

3 In a small bowl, stir together the mayonnaise, lemon zest, and a pinch of salt. Taste, and if you prefer it more lemony, halve the lemon you zested and squeeze some juice into the mayonnaise. Set aside.

4 Place the asparagus spears on the grill directly over the fire and cook, rolling them about a quarter turn every minute or so, until they are just tender and lightly charred, about 5 minutes total.

5 Transfer to a platter and serve at once with the lemon mayonnaise.

Grilled Summer Squash
with Fresh Mint Vinaigrette

4 zucchini, about 1½ lb (750 g) total weight

4 yellow summer squash, about 1½ lb (750 g) total weight

2 tablespoons olive oil, plus more for drizzling

2 tablespoons rice vinegar

½ cup (¾ oz/20 g) chopped fresh mint leaves

Kosher salt and freshly ground pepper

1 tablespoon sesame seeds, toasted

SERVES 6–8

The Game Plan

- Set up grill for direct grilling over medium heat

- Slice squash; coat with oil

- Chop mint

- Grilling time: about 4 minutes

- Dress and season squash

- DON'T FORGET Make sure the squash slices are the same thickness so they cook evenly.

If you have ever planted zucchini or summer squash, you know that at some point you are going to end up with more squashes than you know what to do with. That's the time to pull out this recipe. Grilled summer squashes are splendid on their own, of course. But top them with this simple mint vinaigrette, and you won't mind that garden surplus.

1 Prepare a charcoal or gas grill for direct grilling over medium heat (page 16 or 18). Brush and oil the grill grate.

2 Slice all the squashes crosswise on a sharp diagonal about ½ inch (12 mm) thick. Drizzle with olive oil and toss to coat evenly.

3 Place the squash on the grill directly over the fire and cook, turning, until nicely grill-marked on all sides, about 2 minutes on each side.

4 Transfer the squash pieces to a large bowl. Add the 2 tablespoons oil, the vinegar, and mint, and toss to coat evenly. Season with salt and pepper. Sprinkle with the sesame seeds and serve at once.

Grilled Romaine Salad

FOR THE CAESAR VINAIGRETTE

¼ cup (2 fl oz/60 ml) white wine vinegar

½ teaspoon *each* anchovy paste and whole-grain mustard

1 tablespoon fresh lemon juice

1 tablespoon fresh oregano

¼ teaspoon roasted garlic, homemade (page 145) or store-bought

½ cup (4 fl oz/125 ml) *each* canola oil and extra-virgin olive oil

1 teaspoon honey

Kosher salt and freshly ground pepper

2 heads romaine lettuce, outer leaves removed

Olive oil for drizzling

1 cup (6 oz/185 g) cherry tomatoes, halved

1 avocado, pitted, peeled, and sliced

¼ lb (125 g) Asiago cheese

SERVES 4

The Game Plan

- Make vinaigrette
- Set up grill for direct grilling over medium heat
- Prepare lettuce for grilling
- Grilling time: 4–5 minutes
- Assemble salads
- DON'T FORGET Leave the stem attached so the leaves hold together.

The first time a friend tried to convince me that grilling lettuce was a good idea, I thought she had lost her mind. But I was so wrong. Romaine is both sturdy enough and flavorful enough to stand up to the heat and the char of a grill. Add some avocado and a Caesar-inspired vinaigrette, and you've got a grilled salad that belongs alongside a thick, juicy grilled steak.

1 To make the vinaigrette, add the vinegar, anchovy paste, mustard, lemon juice, oregano, and roasted garlic to a blender or food processor. Pulse to blend. With the machine running, slowly add both oils and process until the dressing emulsifies. Transfer to a bowl, stir in the honey, and season with salt and pepper. You should have about 1¼ cups (10 fl oz/310 ml), which is more than you'll need for this salad; store any extra in an airtight container in the refrigerator for up to 1 week.

2 Prepare a charcoal or gas grill for direct grilling over medium heat (page 16 or 18). Brush and oil the grill grate.

3 Cut each romaine head in half lengthwise. Trim the base of the stem from each half, but leave the remainder of the stem attached. It holds the leaves together. Drizzle the cut side of each half with a little olive oil.

4 Place the romaine halves, cut side down, on the grill directly over the fire and cook until the leaves develop a little char and have begun to wilt, 2–3 minutes. Turn and cook for about 2 minutes more. You want the lettuce to be a little wilted but still hold its shape.

5 Transfer the romaine halves, cut side up, to individual plates, and garnish each plate with one-fourth of the tomatoes and avocado. Using a vegetable peeler, shave the cheese over the salads. Spoon some of the vinaigrette over each salad and serve at once, passing additional vinaigrette at the table.

Grilled Eggplant with Feta

FOR THE FETA DRESSING

¼ cup (2 oz/60 g) Greek-style plain yogurt

1 tablespoon mayonnaise

¼ cup (1½ oz/45 g) crumbled feta cheese

1 tablespoon fresh lemon juice

8 large fresh basil leaves, finely shredded

3 cloves garlic, finely chopped

Hot-pepper sauce

Kosher salt and freshly ground pepper

About 2 tablespoons buttermilk or whole milk, if needed

2 eggplants, cut crosswise into slices ½ inch (12 mm) thick

2 tablespoons canola oil or olive oil

SERVES 4–6

When eggplants are cooked on a grill over a hot fire, they take on an intense smokiness without a touch of bitterness. Here, I've dressed them with classic Mediterranean ingredients that are bold enough to handle the heady aroma and flavor of the eggplant.

1 To make the dressing, in a bowl, stir together the yogurt, mayonnaise, feta, lemon juice, basil, garlic, and 1 or 2 dashes hot-pepper sauce. Season with salt and pepper. Using the buttermilk, thin the sauce to the desired consistency. I like it thick and chunky, almost like a dip.

2 Prepare a charcoal or gas grill for direct grilling over medium heat (page 16 or 18). Brush and oil the grill grate.

3 Generously brush the eggplant slices on both sides with the oil. Place the eggplant slices on the grill directly over the fire and cook, turning once, until the slices are tender but still hold their shape, about 6 minutes on each side.

4 Transfer the eggplant slices to a platter and spoon the dressing over the top. Serve at once.

The Game Plan

- Make dressing
- Set up grill for direct grilling over medium heat
- Slice eggplants and brush with oil
- Grilling time: about 12 minutes
- DON'T FORGET Coat the eggplant slices with plenty of oil so they don't stick to the grill grate.

Stuffed Portobello Mushrooms

4 large portobello mushrooms

FOR THE MARINADE

½ cup (4 fl oz/125 ml) extra-virgin olive oil

¼ cup (2 fl oz/60 ml) balsamic vinegar

¼ cup (⅓ oz/10 g) chopped fresh flat-leaf parsley

3 cloves garlic, pressed

Kosher salt and freshly ground pepper

¼ cup (2 fl oz/60 ml) olive oil, plus more for drizzling

4 cloves garlic, sliced

10 oz (315 g) baby spinach

Kosher salt and freshly ground pepper

½ lb (250 g) fresh goat cheese

½ cup (3 oz/90 g) diced cooked country ham or prosciutto (optional)

SERVES 4 AS A MAIN COURSE OR 8 AS AN APPETIZER

The Game Plan

- Prepare mushrooms
- Make marinade; marinate mushrooms for 2 hours
- Make stuffing
- Set up grill for direct grilling over medium heat
- Stuff mushrooms
- Grilling time: 5–10 minutes
- DON'T FORGET Cover the grill so the mushrooms cook evenly (you don't flip them).

The best way to get committed carnivores to become vegetarians for at least one meal is to serve them steaklike grilled portobello mushrooms. Like all mushrooms, portobellos are sponges, here readily soaking up the flavor of olive oil, vinegar, and herbs. If you like, you can swap out the spinach for Swiss chard or collard greens, and the goat cheese for fontina or Taleggio.

1 Remove the stem from each mushroom. Using a small spoon, carefully scrape away the dark brown gills from the mushroom caps.

2 To make the marinade, in a small bowl, whisk together the ½ cup extra-virgin olive oil, the vinegar, parsley, garlic, and ½ teaspoon each salt and pepper. Place the mushroom caps, hollow side up, in a baking dish. (You will probably need to use 2 baking dishes.) Whisk the marinade briefly to recombine, then pour it evenly over the mushrooms. Let stand at room temperature for 2 hours.

3 Meanwhile, in a large sauté pan over medium heat, warm the ¼ cup olive oil. When it starts to shimmer, throw in the garlic. Turn down the heat slightly and let the oil absorb the flavor of the garlic for about 2 minutes. Add the spinach and, using tongs, constantly move the spinach around until lightly wilted, about 1 minute. Remove from the heat, season with salt and pepper, and set aside.

4 Prepare a charcoal or gas grill for direct grilling over medium heat (page 16 or 18). Brush and oil the grill grate.

5 Divide the spinach mixture evenly among the 4 mushroom caps. Crumble the goat cheese evenly over the filled mushrooms, then top with the ham, if using, again dividing evenly. Drizzle the mushrooms with a little olive oil.

6 Using a large, wide spatula, place the stuffed mushrooms on the grill directly over the fire. Cover the grill, and cook for about 5 minutes. Uncover and check for doneness by pushing on the sides of the mushrooms; they should feel spongy. If they don't feel spongy, re-cover and continue cooking. They will probably take a little longer than 5 minutes but rarely more than 10 minutes.

7 Using the spatula, transfer the mushrooms to a platter. If serving as an appetizer, cut each mushroom into quarters. Serve at once.

Grilled Baby Artichokes
with Spicy Garlic Butter

4 wooden skewers (optional)

4 tablespoons (2 oz/60 g) unsalted butter

3 cloves garlic, minced

2 tablespoons fresh lemon juice

⅛ teaspoon red pepper flakes, or more to taste

Hot-pepper sauce

Kosher salt and freshly ground black pepper

8 baby artichokes (choose larger baby artichokes, not the very small ones), about 1 lb (500 g) total weight

SERVES 4

The Game Plan

- Set up grill for direct grilling over medium heat
- Make garlic butter
- Prepare artichokes for grilling
- Grilling time: 30–35 minutes
- Brush artichokes with butter during grilling
- DON'T FORGET Brush the artichoke hearts often with the garlic butter to infuse them with flavor.

One of the best things you will ever taste is a leaf popped from a perfectly steamed artichoke and dipped in melted butter—that is, until you taste these butter-swabbed grilled artichokes. When you read through the recipe, you might think that they are on the grill too long, but they aren't. Once you strip away the burnt outer leaves, you'll find a fork-tender center.

1 Prepare a charcoal or gas grill for direct grilling over medium heat (page 16 or 18). Brush and oil the grill grate. Soak the skewers in water for at least 30 minutes, if using. (Skewering the artichokes isn't necessary, but it does make life easier.)

2 In a small saucepan over medium-low heat, melt the butter. Add the garlic, lemon juice, red pepper flakes, and 1 or 2 dashes hot-pepper sauce and stir to mix. Season to taste with salt and pepper. Reserve the mixture over low heat.

3 Bang each baby artichoke on a countertop a couple of times. This will loosen the outer leaves and let the butter mixture penetrate better. Then, cut the artichokes in half lengthwise, trim the stems, and using a small spoon, scoop out the hairy choke. Slide the artichoke halves onto the skewers, if using, with the cut sides all facing the same way.

4 Place the artichokes, cut side down, on the grill directly over the fire and cook for about 5 minutes. Brush with the butter mixture and cook for another 5 minutes. Turn the artichokes, brush the cut side with the butter mixture, and continue cooking, turning and brushing with the butter mixture about every 5 minutes, for 20–25 minutes longer, taking care not to burn the artichokes. The artichokes are done if when you press into the middle of the cut side it gives easily.

5 Transfer the artichokes to a platter and pour any remaining butter mixture over them. To eat the artichokes, peel off the tough first layer or two of leaves. Everything else will be nice, tender, and wonderful.

Smoky Grilled Potatoes

8 medium-sized red-skinned or Yukon gold potatoes, about 2½ lb (1.25 kg) total weight

1 tablespoon smoked paprika

⅛ teaspoon granulated garlic

Kosher salt and freshly ground pepper

Olivo oil for drizzling

1 teaspoon fresh thyme leaves

SERVES 4–6

The Game Plan

- Set up grill for direct grilling over medium heat

- Cut potatoes, then season and toss with oil

- Grilling time: about 10 minutes

- DON'T FORGET Be careful when flipping the potato slices as they can easily slip through the grates.

Smoked paprika from Spain has been steadily gaining popularity on the grilling circuit, turning up on meats, poultry, seafood, vegetables, and in sauces. Combined with garlic, thyme, and a hint of salt and pepper, it delivers a smoky accent to these addictive potatoes, which pick up even more smoke on the grill.

1 Prepare a charcoal or gas grill for direct grilling over medium heat (page 16 or 18). Brush and oil the grill grate.

2 Cut each potato into rounds about ½ inch (12 mm) thick. Place in a bowl, add the paprika, granulated garlic, a couple of pinches of salt, and a few grinds of pepper. Toss to coat evenly. Drizzle with olive oil and toss again.

3 Place the potato rounds on the grill directly over the fire and cook, turning once, until lightly charred and tender, about 5 minutes on each side. During the last minute or so of cooking, sprinkle the potatoes with the thyme.

4 Transfer the potatoes to a platter. Serve hot or at room temperature.

Grilled Pineapple Skewers
with Chile-Lime Salt

FOR THE CHILE-LIME SALT

2 tablespoons coarse sea salt

⅛ teaspoon cayenne pepper

Finely grated zest of 1 lime

4–6 wooden skewers

1 pineapple

Olive oil for drizzling

SERVES 4

The Game Plan

- Make chile-lime salt; soak skewers in water for 30 minutes

- Set up grill for direct grilling over medium heat

- Cut pineapple into chunks, then season and thread onto skewers

- Grilling time: 8 minutes

- DON'T FORGET Don't turn the skewers too often—you want them to develop grill marks.

Pineapple develops a smoky sweetness on the grill. The addition of the chile-lime salt both before the skewers go on the grill and just before serving balances that sweetness with a bit of spicy heat, acidity, and tartness. These skewers are absolutely great alongside just about every kind of meat, poultry, and fish. Double the recipe if you're serving a crowd—these tend to go fast.

1 To make the chile-lime salt, in a small bowl, combine the salt, cayenne pepper, and lime zest and mash together with the back of a spoon. Cover and let sit at room temperature for about 30 minutes before using. (The recipe can be doubled or tripled and stored in an airtight container in the refrigerator for up to 2 weeks.) Soak the skewers in water for at least 30 minutes.

2 Prepare a charcoal or gas grill for direct grilling over medium heat (page 16 or 18). Brush and oil the grill grate.

3 Using a serrated knife, cut off the top and bottom from the pineapple. Stand the pineapple upright on a cutting board and slice off the skin in long strips. Lay the pineapple on its side and, using the tip of the knife, cut out the brown "eyes." Cut the pineapple lengthwise into quarters, then cut away the core from each quarter. Slice the quarters crosswise 1 inch (2.5 cm) thick, then cut the slices into 1-inch chunks.

4 Place the pineapple chunks in a bowl, sprinkle with about 2 teaspoons of the chile-lime salt, and toss to coat evenly. Thread the chunks on the skewers and drizzle on all sides with the oil.

5 Place the skewers on the grill directly over the fire and cook, turning as needed, for about 2 minutes on each side, for a total of 8 minutes. Let the pineapple develop a bit of char, which will add to the sweetness.

6 Transfer the skewers to a platter and sprinkle with the remaining chile-lime salt. Serve at once.

Maple-Glazed Peaches
with Toasted Almonds

4 firm, ripe peaches

Olive oil for brushing

1 tablespoon sugar

1 tablespoon pure maple syrup, preferably grade B

2 tablespoons sliced almonds, lightly toasted

Vanilla ice cream for serving (optional)

SERVES 4

The Game Plan

- Set up grill for direct grilling over medium heat

- Halve and pit peaches; brush with oil and sprinkle with sugar

- Grilling time: about 6 minutes

- Drizzle with maple syrup and garnish with almonds

- DON'T FORGET Grill the peach halves cut side down until the flesh is caramelized, then turn them over to finish.

With the exception of pineapple, many folks don't think fruit belongs on a grill. That attitude has them missing a wealth of flavors, as these grilled peaches, their surfaces richly caramelized by a hot fire, illustrate. Leave off the almonds and ice cream and the peaches are a great side to grilled pork chops or tenderloin.

1 Prepare a charcoal or gas grill for direct grilling over medium heat (page 16 or 18). Brush and oil the grill grate.

2 Halve and pit the peaches. Brush all sides with a little olive oil. Sprinkle the cut sides with the sugar, dividing it evenly.

3 Place the peach halves, cut side down, on the grill directly over the fire. Cover the grill and cook for about 2 minutes. Uncover, rotate the peaches about 45 degrees, and cook for 1 minute more. Turn the peaches, re-cover the grill, and cook until they are slightly softened but still hold their shape, about 3 minutes longer.

4 Transfer the peach halves to individual plates or bowls. Drizzle the maple syrup over the peaches, dividing it evenly. Garnish with the almonds, again dividing evenly, and top with ice cream, if desired. Serve at once.

How to grill the perfect
Pizza

Nowadays, outdoor kitchens are all the rage, with many of them including a wood-burning pizza oven in the mix. Put your money elsewhere. Your grill is the perfect pizza "oven." The fire gives the crust a nice crackle and char and the toppings a smoky flavor.

MAKE YOUR OWN DOUGH Most folks judge a good pizza by its dough. Making your own is rewarding and fairly simple. If you are rushed for time, frozen dough and dough purchased at a pizzeria are good alternatives. Refrigerated dough is usually not as successful unless it comes from a high-end market.

CHOOSE THE TOPPINGS The recipe here is for classic pizza Margherita, but don't let that hinder your creativity. Just remember the best pizza joints always use top-quality ingredients, and you should, too.

WAIT FOR THE HEAT Be patient and let the grill get as hot as possible. You may want cooler conditions after you flip the crust, but you want a hot fire to start.

DUST THE BAKER'S PEEL WITH CORNMEAL Be sure you dust the baker's peel—or the back of a rimless baking sheet—with cornmeal before you slide the dough round onto it for transport to the grill. The grains of cornmeal act like ball bearings, helping to slide the dough easily over the fire. The cornmeal also adds some crunch.

DON'T RUSH THE GRILLING Once the dough round is on the grill, let it set up and become firm on the underside before you turn it. Then, use the peel, the baking sheet, a large spatula, or tongs to flip it.

WORK QUICKLY You need to work quickly to get your toppings on the crust and get the grill lid closed to maintain the heat. As soon as the cheese is bubbly, your pizza is ready.

Grilled Pizza Margherita

Foolproof Pizza Dough
(page 185)

Bread flour for dusting

Olive oil for brushing

Cornmeal for dusting

2 cups (16 fl oz/500 ml) marinara
sauce or 30–40 plum tomatoes,
cored and thinly sliced

1½ lb (750 g) fresh mozzarella
cheese, thinly sliced, or
low-moisture whole-milk
mozzarella cheese, shredded

2 cups (3 oz/90 g) torn fresh
basil leaves

2 cloves garlic, finely chopped

Kosher salt and freshly
ground pepper

1 Make the pizza dough as directed through Step 1.

2 Prepare a charcoal or gas grill for direct grilling over medium-high heat (page 16 or 18). Brush and oil the grill grate.

3 Dump the dough onto a floured work surface, then divide into 4 equal portions. Using a floured rolling pin, roll out each portion into a round about 8 inches (20 cm) in diameter and ⅛ inch (3 mm) thick. Brush the edge of each round with olive oil.

4 Slide 1 round onto a baker's peel or the underside of a baking sheet dusted with cornmeal, and then carefully slide the round off the peel onto the grill directly over the fire. Repeat with the remaining 3 rounds. Cook the crusts until the underside is well marked, about 2 minutes. Using the peel, transfer the crusts, grilled side up, back to the work surface.

5 Top each crust with one-fourth of the sauce or tomato slices, then top with one-fourth each of the cheese, basil, and garlic. Season with salt and pepper. Using the peel, return the topped crusts to the grill, cover the grill, and cook until each crust is firm and browned at the edges and the cheese has melted a bit, 4–6 minutes.

6 Transfer the pizzas to a cutting board, cut into wedges, and serve at once.

SERVES 4

Alsatian Pizza
with Bacon and Caramelized Onions

FOR THE FOOLPROOF PIZZA DOUGH

⅔ cup (5 fl oz/160 ml) warm water (105°–115°F/40°–46°C)

1 package (2½ teaspoons) active dry yeast

½ teaspoon sugar

2 cups (10 oz/315 g) bread flour, plus more for dusting

2 tablespoons extra-virgin olive oil, plus more for oiling

Kosher salt and freshly ground pepper

3 tablespoons unsalted butter

2 yellow onions, thinly sliced

1 tablespoon firmly packed light brown sugar

8 slices thick-cut applewood-smoked bacon, cut into strips

Cornmeal for dusting

¼ lb (125 g) Gruyère cheese, thinly sliced

2 tablespoons chopped fresh thyme

SERVES 4

The Game Plan

- Make pizza dough; let rise for 1–1½ hours; meanwhile, cook onions and bacon
- Set up grill for direct grilling over medium-high heat
- Roll out dough
- Grill undersides of pizzas; flip and add toppings
- Grilling time: 6–8 minutes

This French-inspired pizza makes a good first course, great party food, or even a satisfying main with a green salad on the side. Don't worry if your kids ask, "Where's the tomato sauce?" Once they try a slice of this pie, they'll be sold on the marriage of crisp bacon, nutty Gruyère, and sweet onions.

1 To make the pizza dough, in a bowl, whisk together the water, yeast, and sugar. Let stand until foamy, about 5 minutes. Add the flour, oil, 1 teaspoon salt, and ½ teaspoon pepper. Stir until the dough pulls away from the sides of the bowl. Pull the dough out onto a floured work surface and knead a few times, then form into a ball. Oil a second bowl, put the ball in the bowl, and turn to coat it with oil. Cover the bowl with plastic wrap and set aside in a warm, draft-free area. Let the dough rise until doubled in size, 1–1½ hours.

2 While the dough is rising, in a sauté pan over medium heat, melt the butter. Add the onions and stir to coat. Sprinkle the sugar over the onions and stir once more. Reduce the heat to medium-low and cook, stirring, until the onions are golden brown, about 20 minutes. Transfer to a bowl.

3 At the same time, in a second sauté pan over medium heat, cook the bacon, stirring, until crisp, about 8 minutes. Transfer to paper towels to drain.

4 Prepare a charcoal or gas grill for direct grilling over medium-high heat (page 16 or 18). Brush and oil the grill grate.

5 Dump the dough onto a floured work surface, then divide in half. Using a floured rolling pin, roll out 1 half into a round 10–12 inches (25–30 cm) in diameter and about ⅛ inch (3 mm) thick. Repeat with the second half.

6 Slide 1 round onto a baker's peel or a rimless baking sheet dusted with cornmeal, and then carefully slide the round off the peel onto the grill directly over the fire. Repeat with the second round. Cook the crusts until the underside is well marked, about 2 minutes. Using the peel, transfer the crusts, grilled side up, back to the work surface.

7 Top each crust with half the onions, half the bacon, and then half the cheese. Season with salt and pepper. Using the peel, return the topped crusts to the grill, cover the grill, and cook until each crust is firm and browned at the edges and the cheese has melted a bit, 4–6 minutes.

8 Transfer the pizzas to a cutting board and sprinkle with the thyme. Cut into wedges and serve at once.

Cheesesteak Piadine

Foolproof Pizza Dough
(page 185)

1 tablespoon unsalted butter

1 tablespoon canola oil

2 red bell peppers, seeded and
cut lengthwise into narrow strips

2 sweet onions, thinly sliced

1 lb (500 g) top sirloin or rib eye
steak, frozen for 30 minutes, then
sliced very thinly

Kosher salt and freshly
ground pepper

Cornmeal for dusting

½ lb (250 g) provolone cheese,
thinly sliced

SERVES 4

The Game Plan

- Make pizza dough; let rise
  for 1–1½ hours

- Freeze steak for 30 minutes
  then slice thinly; slice
  peppers, onions, and cheese

- Set up grill for direct grilling
  over medium-high heat

- Set pan on grill; cook steak,
  peppers, and onions

- Roll out dough

- Grill undersides of crusts;
  flip, add toppings, then fold

- Grilling time: about 6 minutes

- DON'T FORGET Use a large,
  wide spatula to fold the
  rounds in half.

Basically, these are Philly cheesesteak sandwiches made with grilled homemade flatbread instead of French rolls. Purists insist on just thinly sliced steak and melted cheese for the filling, but I like to add onions and bell peppers, too. This recipe is easily doubled—you already have enough dough—to feed a crowd.

1 Make the pizza dough as directed through Step 1.

2 Prepare a charcoal or gas grill for direct grilling over medium-high heat (page 16 or 18). Brush and oil the grill grate.

3 A paella pan is perfect for what you are about to do. If you don't own one, a large cast-iron frying pan or rimmed baking sheet works well, too. Add the butter and oil to the pan and place on the grill directly over the fire. When the butter begins to foam, add the peppers and onions and cook until wilted, about 5 minutes. Add the meat and season with salt and pepper. Cook, tossing and turning, until the meat no longer looks raw, 2–3 minutes. Remove the pan from the grill and cover with foil to keep warm.

4 Dump the dough onto a floured work surface, then divide in half. Refrigerate or freeze half for another use. Divide the remaining half in half again. Using a floured rolling pin, roll out each half into a round 8–10 inches (20–25 cm) in diameter and about ⅛ inch (3 mm) thick.

5 Slide 1 round onto a baker's peel or rimless baking sheet dusted with cornmeal, and then carefully slide the round off the peel onto the grill directly over the fire. Repeat with the remaining round. Cook the crusts until the underside is well marked, about 2 minutes. Flip the rounds, and then working quickly, divide half of the cheese slices between the 2 rounds, placing it in the center of each round. Top the cheese on each round with half of the beef mixture, then top the beef mixture with the remaining cheese, dividing it evenly. Cook for 2 minutes longer, then, using a large, wide spatula, fold each round in half, enclosing the filling. Continue to cook until the cheese has melted, about 2 minutes longer.

6 Transfer the folded rounds to a cutting board, cut in half, and serve.

Poblano and Jack Quesadillas

4 poblano chiles

8 flour tortillas, each 10 inches (25 cm) in diameter

½ lb (250 g) pepper jack cheese, shredded

Creamy Avocado Salsa (page 215) and/or Smoky Tomato Salsa (page 214) for serving

SERVES 4 AS A MAIN COURSE OR 8 AS AN APPETIZER

The Game Plan

- Make salsa(s); refrigerate
- Set up grill for direct grilling over medium-high heat
- Shred cheese
- Grill chiles for 4–5 minutes; cut into strips
- Assemble quesadillas
- Grilling time: 6–7 minutes
- DON'T FORGET Leave an empty border around the edges of the tortillas so the filling doesn't spill out.

Quesadillas are a popular finger food that everybody seems to like. Cook them on the grill, and everybody will like them even better. I often serve them as an appetizer with a couple of my classic salsas. That way, my guests can happily nibble away on the cheese-and-chile-filled wedges while I ready the main course.

1 Prepare a charcoal or gas grill for direct grilling over medium-high heat (page 16 or 18). Brush and oil the grill grate.

2 Place the poblano chiles on the grill directly over the fire and cook, turning as needed, until charred on all sides, 4–5 minutes. Transfer to a work surface and let cool until they can be handled. Peel, stem, seed, and cut lengthwise into narrow strips.

3 Place 4 of the tortillas on 2 baking sheets. Divide the chile strips and cheese evenly among them, leaving a ½-inch (12-mm) border around the edge of the tortilla. Top each with a second tortilla.

4 Using 1 or 2 large, wide spatulas, transfer each quesadilla to the grill directly over the fire. Cook for about 3 minutes, pressing on the top tortilla of each quesadilla with a spatula so that the tortillas will meld. Flip each quesadilla and cook until the cheese is melted and the tortillas are golden brown, 3–4 minutes.

5 Transfer to a cutting board and cut each quesadilla into 6 wedges. Serve at once with the salsa(s).

Grilled Panzanella Salad

½ cup (4 oz/125 g)
unsalted butter

2 cloves garlic, finely chopped

1 loaf (1 lb/500 g) day-old
country-style bread, cut into
slices ¾ inch (2 cm) thick

6 dead-ripe, meaty tomatoes,
preferably an assortment of
heirloom varieties, cored and
cut into chunks

¼ cup (1½ oz/45 g) finely
chopped red onion

⅓ cup (3 fl oz/80 ml) extra-
virgin olive oil

2 tablespoons balsamic vinegar

2 tablespoons chopped
fresh basil

1 tablespoon chopped
fresh tarragon

Kosher salt and freshly
ground pepper

¼ lb (125 g) feta cheese,
crumbled

SERVES 6–8

The Game Plan

- Set up grill for direct grilling
  over medium heat

- Melt butter; slice bread;
  brush with butter

- Grilling time: 2–4 minutes

- Cube bread and cut
  tomatoes; assemble salad

- DON'T FORGET Use a sturdy
  bread, preferably stale.

The Italian bread-and-tomato salad known as panzanella is one of the best ways that I know of to use up day-old bread. And if you char both the bread and the tomatoes on the grill, this popular salad tastes even better. Save this recipe for summertime, when flavorful heirloom tomatoes are in the market. This dish practically begs for grill-roasted chicken or grilled flank steak.

1 Prepare a charcoal or gas grill for direct grilling over medium heat (page 16 or 18). Brush and oil the grill grate.

2 In a small saucepan over medium heat, melt the butter. Throw in the garlic and cook it for 2–3 minutes so it takes on a bit of color. Remove from the heat and brush the garlic butter on both sides of each bread slice.

3 Place the bread on the grill directly over the fire and cover the grill. Toast the bread, turning once, until well marked and slightly charred. Don't stray from the grill. Depending on the moisture content of the bread, this could take 2 minutes total, though it usually takes about 4 minutes.

4 Transfer the bread to a large cutting board and cut into roughly bite-sized cubes. Throw the cubes into a large serving bowl. Add the tomatoes, onion, oil, vinegar, basil, tarragon, ½ teaspoon salt, and 8–10 grinds pepper. Fold gently to combine. Your hands are good tools for this step. Taste and adjust with salt and pepper, if you like.

5 Sprinkle the feta over the top and serve at room temperature.

Bruschetta
with Three Toppings

2 cups (12 oz/375 g) chopped tomatoes and/or quartered cherry tomatoes

4 cloves garlic, finely minced

1 tablespoon chopped fresh basil

Kosher salt and freshly ground pepper

Extra-virgin olive oil

3 tablespoons unsalted butter

1 lb (500 g) cremini mushrooms, sliced

1 shallot, finely chopped

¼ cup (2 fl oz/60 ml) red wine vinegar

1 cup (8 fl oz/250 ml) low-sodium beef broth

4 fresh thyme sprigs

Grilled Balsamic Onions (page 200), chopped

1 teaspoon chopped fresh sage

12 slices country-style bread, such as sourdough batard

¼ cup (1 oz/30 g) grated Parmesan cheese

1 lb (500 g) fresh mozzarella cheese, cut into thin slices

SERVES 6–12

The Game Plan

- Make tomato topping
- Make mushroom topping
- Set up grill for direct grilling over medium heat
- Make balsamic onions
- Grill bread 2 minutes per side; assemble bruschetta

Bruschetta, which is simply grilled bread topped with something, is the ideal party food: easy to make, serve, and eat. I've put together three toppings—classic tomato, garlic, and basil; sautéed mushrooms with Parmesan; and grilled balsamic onions with mozzarella—that are guaranteed crowd-pleasers. Sprinkle with fresh herbs and drizzle with a little olive oil just before serving.

1 To make the tomato topping, in a bowl, mix together the tomatoes, half the garlic, and the basil and season with salt and pepper. Add a glug of oil and toss to mix, then set aside. (The topping can be made up to 2 days in advance and refrigerated.)

2 To make the mushroom topping, in a large sauté pan over medium heat, melt the butter. When the butter foams, add the mushrooms, toss to coat, and then cook for 4–5 minutes without stirring. Turn and cook for 4–5 minutes longer. Be patient. You want the mushrooms to be golden brown and slightly crisp. Do not salt. Transfer the mushrooms to a bowl. Return the pan to medium heat and add a little oil. When it shimmers, add the shallot and cook until softened, about 2 minutes. Add the remaining 2 cloves minced garlic and cook for another minute. Return the mushrooms to the pan, add the vinegar, and cook until reduced, about 3 minutes. Add the broth and thyme and cook until the liquid has almost evaporated, 5–8 minutes. Remove from the heat, remove and discard the thyme sprigs, and set aside. (The mushroom mixture can be made up to 3 days in advance and refrigerated.)

3 Prepare a charcoal or gas grill for direct grilling over medium heat (page 16 or 18). Brush and oil the grill grate.

4 To make the onion topping, prepare the grilled balsamic onions. Combine the balsamic onions and sage and toss to mix.

5 Place the bread slices on the grill directly over the fire and cook, turning once, until toasted and grill marked, about 2 minutes on each side.

6 Transfer the bread slices to platters or trays. Top one-third of the grilled bread slices with the tomato topping. Top half of the remaining grilled bread slices with the mushroom mixture, then sprinkle evenly with Parmesan and return to the grill until the cheese starts to sweat, 2–3 minutes. Top the remaining grilled bread slices with the mozzarella and onion mixture and return to the grill until the cheese softens, about 3 minutes. Serve at once.

Smoky Baked Beans with Bacon

1 lb (500 g) thick-cut sliced applewood-smoked bacon

2 large cans (32 oz/1 kg *each*) Great Northern, navy, or cannellini beans

1 can (15 oz/470 g) *each* black beans and kidney beans

1 yellow onion, finely chopped

½ cup (4 fl oz/125 ml) of your favorite BBQ sauce, homemade (page 212) or store-bought

½ cup (5½ oz/170 g) dark maple syrup

½ cup (5 oz/155 g) dark brown sugar

3 tablespoons prepared yellow mustard

1 teaspoon dry mustard

Kosher salt and freshly ground pepper

SERVES 10–12

1 Preheat the oven to 350°F (180°C).

2 In a large frying pan over medium heat, fry half of the bacon until crisp, about 5 minutes. Transfer the bacon to paper towels to drain and cool, then crumble. Reserve the crumbled bacon and the bacon drippings separately.

3 Drain and rinse all the beans. In a 9-by-13-inch (23-by-33-cm) baking dish with at least 3-inch (7.5-cm) sides, stir together all the beans, the onion, BBQ sauce, maple syrup, brown sugar, both mustards, and crumbled bacon. Lay the uncooked bacon slices in a single layer over the top of the mixture and cover the dish with aluminum foil.

4 Bake for 45 minutes. Uncover and continue to bake until thickened, about 1 hour more. Remove from the oven, season with salt and pepper, and serve hot or at room temperature. The beans taste best when baked a day in advance, cooled, covered, refrigerated, and then reheated in a 350°F (180°C) oven.

Drunken Pinto Beans

2¼ cups (1 lb/500 g) dried pinto beans

3 ribs celery

2 carrots

1 yellow onion

4 fresh thyme sprigs

6 slices thick-cut applewood-smoked bacon, chopped

4 cloves garlic

1 bottle (12 fl oz/375 ml) dark beer such as a porter or stout

Kosher salt and freshly ground pepper

SERVES 10–12

1 Pick over the beans, discarding any misshapen beans or grit, then rinse and place in a large non-reactive bowl. Add water to cover by 3 inches (7.5 cm) and let soak overnight.

2 Cut the celery, carrots, and onion into large chunks. Tie the thyme sprigs together with kitchen twine. Drain the beans and place in a slow cooker or a large, heavy pot over the stovetop. Add the bacon, garlic, celery, carrots, onion, beer, and thyme and stir to mix. Add water to cover the beans by about 1 inch (2.5 cm). If using a slow cooker, cover and cook until tender, on the low setting for about 10 hours or on the high setting for about 6 hours. If using a pot, bring the mixture to a boil over high heat, then reduce the heat to low and cook until tender, about 3 hours.

3 Remove and discard the onion, celery, and carrot chunks and the thyme sprigs. Season the beans with salt and pepper. Serve at once. Or, let cool, cover, and refrigerate for 1 day for the best flavor, then reheat gently to serve.

Southwestern Bean Salad

2 ears cooked husked corn, preferably grilled (page 165)

2 cans (15 oz/470 g *each*) black beans, drained and rinsed

1 can (15 oz/470 g) red kidney beans, drained and rinsed

1 cup (6 oz/185 g) Pico de Gallo (page 215) or Smoky Tomato Salsa (page 214)

2 green onions, thinly sliced

½ cup (¾ oz/20 g) chopped fresh cilantro

Juice of 1 lime

Kosher salt and freshly ground pepper

SERVES 8–10

1 Stand each ear of corn upright over a shallow bowl and, using a chef's knife, cut the kernels from the cob. Transfer the kernels to a large bowl and add the black beans, kidney beans, salsa, and green onions. Stir to mix. Stir in the cilantro, then season with the lime juice, salt, and pepper.

2 Serve at room temperature, or cover and refrigerate for about 2 hours and serve chilled. The salad will keep, covered, for up to 3 days.

Potato Salad

3 lb (1.5 kg) red-skinned potatoes

Kosher salt and freshly ground pepper

3 tablespoons white wine vinegar

1 cup (8 fl oz/250 ml) mayonnaise, preferably homemade (page 216)

2 tablespoons whole-grain mustard

4 ribs celery, finely diced

4 green onions, including tender green parts, chopped

2 tablespoons minced fresh flat-leaf parsley

SERVES 8

1 In a large saucepan, combine the potatoes with salted water to cover, cover the pan, and bring to a boil over high heat. Uncover, reduce the heat to medium-low, and simmer until the potatoes are tender when pierced with a knife, about 25 minutes.

2 Drain the potatoes, then rinse them under cold running water until they are cool enough to handle. Cut the potatoes into chunks about ½ inch (12 mm) thick and place in a large bowl. Sprinkle with the vinegar. Let cool completely.

3 In a small bowl, stir together the mayonnaise and mustard. Add to the cooled potatoes along with the celery, green onions, and parsley and mix gently. Season with salt and pepper.

4 Cover and refrigerate until chilled, at least 2 hours. Serve chilled.

Mac and Cheese

7 tablespoons (3½ oz/105 g) unsalted butter

1 clove garlic, minced

1½ cups (3 oz/90 g) coarse fresh bread crumbs

Kosher salt and freshly ground pepper

1 lb (500 g) elbow macaroni

¼ cup (1½ oz/45 g) all-purpose flour

3 cups (24 fl oz/750 ml) whole milk, heated

2 cups (8 oz/250 g) shredded sharp Cheddar cheese

2 cups (8 oz/250 g) shredded fontina or Gruyère cheese

½ teaspoon dry mustard

SERVES 6

1 In a large frying pan over medium-low heat, melt 3 tablespoons of the butter. Add the garlic and cook, stirring frequently, until tender but not browned, about 3 minutes. Add the bread crumbs and stir until coated with butter. Set aside.

2 Preheat the oven to 350°F (180°C). Butter a shallow 3-qt (3-l) baking dish.

3 Bring a large pot three-fourths full of lightly salted water to a boil over high heat. Add the macaroni, stir well, and cook until not quite al dente, a minute or so less than package directions. (The macaroni will cook again in the oven, so do not overcook it now.) Drain well and set aside.

4 Add the remaining 4 tablespoons (2 oz/60 g) butter to the pot used for the pasta and melt over medium heat. Whisk in the flour, then reduce the heat to medium-low, and let bubble for 1 minute without browning. Gradually whisk in the hot milk, raise the heat to medium, and bring to a boil, whisking frequently. Remove from the heat, stir in both cheeses along with the mustard, and season with salt and pepper. Stir in the pasta, coating evenly. Transfer to the prepared baking dish, spreading evenly, and then sprinkle evenly with the buttered crumbs.

5 Bake until the crumbs are browned and the sauce is bubbling, about 20 minutes. Let cool for 5 minutes before serving.

VARIATION To give your mac and cheese a little personality, add chopped crisply cooked bacon, cubes of smoked ham, cooked green peas, sautéed mushrooms, or crumbled blue cheese.

Coconut Rice

1 tablespoon canola oil

1 large shallot, minced

1 teaspoon peeled and grated fresh ginger

2 cups (14 oz/440 g) jasmine rice, rinsed

1 cup (8 fl oz/250 ml) coconut milk

Kosher salt

½ cup (2 oz/60 g) shredded coconut, toasted (optional)

SERVES 6

1 In a large saucepan over medium-high heat, warm the canola oil. Add the shallot and ginger and sauté until fragrant, about 30 seconds. Add the rice and stir to mix well. Add 2 cups (16 fl oz/500 ml) water, the coconut milk, and 1 teaspoon salt and bring to a boil. Reduce the heat to low, cover, and simmer for 20 minutes.

2 Remove the pan from the heat and let the rice stand, covered, until tender, about 10 minutes longer. Fluff the rice with a fork, stir in the shredded coconut, if using, and serve at once.

Mexican Rice

1 can (14½ oz/455 g) whole tomatoes, drained

3 tablespoons chopped white onion

2 small cloves garlic, chopped

¼ cup (2 fl oz/60 ml) corn oil or canola oil

1 cup (7 oz/220 g) medium-grain white rice

1 can (4 oz/125 g) mild green chiles, drained, seeded, and sliced lengthwise

6 fresh cilantro sprigs, tied together with kitchen string, plus chopped cilantro for garnish

Kosher salt

SERVES 4–6

1 In a blender, combine the tomatoes, onion, and garlic and process until smooth. Set aside.

2 In a saucepan over medium-high heat, warm the oil. When it is hot, add the rice and toast for about 1 minute. Do not allow it to brown. Add the tomato mixture and stir gently to blend. Add 2 cups (16 fl oz/500 ml) hot water and the chiles, cilantro sprigs, and 1 teaspoon salt. Bring to a boil, shaking the pan to mix the ingredients, then reduce the heat to low. Cover and simmer for 10 minutes. Uncover and stir the rice carefully to distribute the liquid evenly (most of it will have been absorbed). Re-cover and simmer until all the liquid is fully absorbed, about 10 minutes longer.

3 Remove from the heat and let stand, covered, for 10 minutes. Uncover, remove and discard the cilantro sprigs, and fluff with a fork. Garnish with chopped cilantro and serve at once.

Herbed Rice Pilaf

2 tablespoons unsalted butter

1 rib celery, finely chopped

1 carrot, peeled and finely chopped

½ small yellow onion, finely chopped

2 cloves garlic, finely chopped

2 fresh thyme sprigs

1 fresh rosemary sprig

1 cup (7 oz/220 g) long-grain white rice or 1 cup (6 oz/185 g) wild and brown rice blend

1½ cups (12 fl oz/375 ml) low-sodium chicken or vegetable broth

Kosher salt and freshly ground pepper

SERVES 4–6

1 In a saucepan over medium heat, melt the butter. Add the celery, carrot, onion, garlic, thyme, and rosemary and sauté until the vegetables have softened, 3–5 minutes. Add the rice and stir to combine. Cook for 1 minute to toast lightly. Pour in the broth (add 1 cup/8 fl oz/250 ml water if using a wild rice blend), and bring to a boil. Give the ingredients a stir, then cover, reduce the heat to low, and cook until the liquid is absorbed and the rice is tender, about 20 minutes for white rice or 40 minutes for the wild rice blend.

2 Remove from the heat and let stand, covered, for 10 minutes. Uncover, remove the herb sprigs, and fluff with a fork. Season with salt and pepper and serve at once.

The Best Mashed Potatoes

3 lb (1.5 kg) russet potatoes, peeled and cut into chunks

Kosher salt and freshly ground white pepper

½ cup (4 oz/125 g) unsalted butter, at room temperature

About ½ cup (4 fl oz/125 ml) whole milk, warmed

3 tablespoons minced fresh chives

SERVES 6

1 In a large saucepan, combine the potatoes with salted water to cover, cover the pan, and bring to a boil over high heat. Uncover, reduce the heat to medium-low, and simmer until the potatoes are tender when pierced with a knife, about 20 minutes. Drain well. Return the potatoes to the pan and stir over medium-low heat for 2 minutes to evaporate the excess moisture.

2 Press the warm potatoes through a ricer into a large bowl. Cut the butter into slices and scatter over the potatoes. Whisk in the butter and enough of the milk to give the potatoes the texture you like. (Or, if you don't have a ricer, beat the potatoes in the pot with a handheld mixer on high speed. Add the butter and continue beating on high speed, adding milk as needed to create the desired texture. Be careful not to overbeat the potatoes.)

3 Mix in the chives and season with salt and pepper. Transfer to a warmed serving bowl and serve at once.

Creamed Spinach

3½ lb (1.75 kg) spinach

1 cup (8 fl oz/250 ml) heavy cream

1 cup (8 fl oz/250 ml) whole milk

3 tablespoons unsalted butter

¼ cup (1½ oz/45 g) minced shallots

1 clove garlic, minced

3 tablespoons all-purpose flour

½ cup (2 oz/60 g) grated Parmesan cheese

Kosher salt and freshly ground pepper

Pinch of freshly grated nutmeg

SERVES 6

1 Remove the stems from the spinach leaves and chop the leaves coarsely. Fill the sink with cold water, add the spinach, and swirl to loosen any grit. Transfer the spinach, with any water clinging to it, to a large bowl.

2 In a large saucepan, bring ½ cup (4 fl oz/125 ml) water to a boil over high heat. In batches, add the spinach and cover, letting each batch wilt before adding the next one. Then cook, stirring occasionally, until tender, about 5 minutes. Drain the spinach in a sieve, then rinse briefly under cold running water. Let cool until it is easy to handle. A handful at a time, squeeze the spinach to remove any excess water and place in a bowl. Set aside.

3 In a small saucepan over medium heat, combine the cream and milk and bring to a simmer. Remove from the heat. In the large saucepan you used for the spinach, melt the butter over medium heat. Add the shallots and garlic and cook, stirring frequently, until the shallots have softened, about 2 minutes. Whisk in the flour, reduce the heat to medium-low, and let bubble for 1 minute without browning. Gradually whisk in the hot cream mixture, raise the heat to medium, and bring to a boil, whisking frequently. Reduce the heat to medium-low and simmer, stirring often, until lightly thickened, about 5 minutes. Stir in the spinach and warm through, about 5 minutes more.

4 Whisk in the Parmesan, then season with salt, pepper, and a pinch of nutmeg. Transfer to a warmed serving dish and serve at once.

Vinegar-Braised Collard Greens

4 lb (2 kg) collard greens

6 slices thick-cut applewood-smoked bacon, coarsely chopped

1 tablespoon canola oil

4 cloves garlic, minced

¼ teaspoon red pepper flakes

2 tablespoons cider vinegar, plus more for serving

Kosher salt

SERVES 6–8

1 Trim off and discard the thick stems from the collard greens. In batches, stack the leaves and cut crosswise into strips about ½ inch (12 mm) wide. Fill the sink with cold water, add the greens, and swirl to loosen any grit. Transfer the collard greens, with any water clinging to them, to a large bowl.

2 In a large pot or a large, deep sauté pan over medium heat, fry the bacon in the oil until browned and crisp, about 8 minutes. Using a slotted spoon, transfer the bacon to paper towels to drain. Remove the pot from the heat, with the bacon fat still in it, and let cool slightly.

3 Return the pot to medium-low heat, add the garlic, and cook, stirring frequently, until softened, about 1 minute. Raise the heat to medium-high, add a handful of the collard greens, cover, and cook until the greens start to wilt. Continue adding the greens a handful at a time, allowing them to wilt before adding the next batch, until all of the greens are in the pot. Add the red pepper flakes, cover, reduce the heat to medium-low, and simmer, stirring occasionally, for about 15 minutes if you like the greens tender but still fresh, or up to 45 minutes if you like them well done.

4 Stir in the bacon and the 2 tablespoons vinegar. Season with salt, then taste and adjust with red pepper flakes. Transfer the greens and their cooking liquid to a warmed serving bowl, and serve at once. Pass additional vinegar at the table.

Cheesy Cauliflower Gratin

1 head cauliflower (about 3 lb/1.5 kg), cored and cut into small florets

Olive oil for drizzling

Kosher salt and freshly ground black pepper

2 tablespoons unsalted butter

2 tablespoons flour

1 cup (8 fl oz/250 ml) whole milk, warmed

1 cup (4 oz/125 g) shredded Gruyère or Cheddar cheese

⅛ teaspoon cayenne pepper

Pinch of ground nutmeg

SERVES 6–8

1 Preheat the oven to 425°F (220°C). Place the cauliflower florets on a rimmed baking sheet and drizzle with a little olive oil. Season with salt and black pepper and toss to coat evenly.

2 Bake the cauliflower, stirring occasionally, until crisp-tender and browned on the edges, 10–15 minutes.

3 Meanwhile, in a saucepan over low heat, melt the butter. Whisk in the flour and cook, stirring constantly, for 2 minutes. Slowly add the warm milk, whisking constantly. Simmer until the mixture starts to thicken, about 2 minutes. Add the cheese and stir until the cheese has melted and the sauce is smooth. Add the cayenne pepper and nutmeg and season with salt.

4 Transfer the cauliflower to a buttered 2-qt (2-l) baking dish. Pour the cheese sauce over the cauliflower and stir to combine. Bake until bubbly and the top is browned, about 20 minutes. Let cool about 5 minutes before serving.

Grilled Balsamic Onions

4–6 wooden skewers

2 red onions, cut into thick rings

¼ cup (2 fl oz/60 ml)
balsamic vinegar

SERVES 4

1 Prepare a charcoal or gas grill for direct grilling over medium heat (page 16 or 18). Brush and oil the grill grate. Soak the wooden skewers in water for at least 30 minutes.

2 Slide a skewer horizontally through the midpoint of each onion slice. This will ensure the slices hold together and will make turning them on the grill easier. You should be able to fit 2 slices on each skewer.

3 Place the onions on the grill directly over the fire and cook, turning once, for 4–5 minutes on each side. You want the onions nicely charred, but you also want them to still have a little of the red coloring.

4 Slide the onion slices off the skewers into a bowl and separate the slices into rings. Immediately add the vinegar and toss the onions to coat evenly. Let stand, tossing occasionally, for at least 30 minutes before using.

Balsamic Onion and Green Bean Salad

Grilled Balsamic Onions
(see above)

1½–2 lb (750 g–1 kg)
green beans

1 tablespoon fresh tarragon or
1 teaspoon dried tarragon

Olive oil for drizzling

Kosher salt and freshly
ground pepper

¼ cup (⅓ oz/10 g) chopped
fresh flat-leaf parsley

SERVES 6–8

1 Prepare the grilled onions, chop, and let sit for 30 minutes as directed.

2 Meanwhile, bring a large saucepan three-fourths full of water to a boil. Add the green beans and cook until just tender, about 5 minutes. Drain and immerse in ice water to halt the cooking. Drain again, pat dry with paper towels, and place in a serving bowl.

3 Add the onions and tarragon and toss to mix. Drizzle with a little olive oil, season with salt and pepper, then add the parsley, and toss again. Serve at room temperature, or cover and refrigerate for about 2 hours and serve chilled.

VARIATION This salad is especially delicious with some chopped crisply cooked bacon or chopped or shredded proscuitto added right before serving.

Grilled Veggies

2 red onions, thickly sliced

2 large red bell peppers, stemmed, seeded, and cut into thick strips

3 large tomatoes, halved crosswise

3 Japanese eggplants, cut lengthwise into slices about ½ inch (12 mm) thick

2 zucchini, trimmed and halved lengthwise

Kosher salt and freshly ground black pepper

Olive oil for drizzling

Balsamic vinegar for drizzling (optional)

SERVES 4–8

1 Prepare a charcoal or gas grill for direct grilling over medium heat (page 16 or 18). Brush and oil the grill grate.

2 Arrange all of the vegetables on a large rimmed baking sheet. Sprinkle with salt and pepper, and drizzle with some olive oil. Toss to coat lightly.

3 Place the onion slices and peppers, skin side down, over the hottest part of the grill. Cook the onions, turning once, for 4–5 minutes on each side. You want the onions slightly charred, but to hold their shape. Grill the peppers until the skins are blackened, 8–10 minutes. Transfer to a platter.

4 Grill the eggplant and zucchini, turning once, until lightly charred and tender when pierced with a knife, about 8 minutes total. Grill the tomatoes, turning once, until charred on all sides and starting to soften, 5–8 minutes total. Transfer to a platter.

5 Drizzle the vegetables with more olive oil and some balsamic vinegar, if desired. Season to taste with salt and pepper and serve at once.

Pesto Pasta Salad

Kosher salt

1 lb (500 g) penne or other short tube pasta

1 cup (6 oz/185 g) halved cherry tomatoes, preferably a mixture of red and yellow

½ cup (4 fl oz/125 ml) pesto, homemade (page 213) or store-bought, plus more as needed

SERVES 6–8

1 Bring a large pot three-fourths full of salted water to a boil. Add the pasta, stir well, and cook until al dente, according to package directions. Reserve ½ cup (4 fl oz/125 ml) of the pasta water. Drain the pasta in a colander, rinse with cold running water, and drain again.

2 Transfer the pasta to a large bowl, add the tomatoes and the pesto, and stir to combine. Add a little of the reserved pasta water to loosen the sauce, and more pesto as you like, to taste. Serve at room temperature.

Creamy Coleslaw

1 head green cabbage
(about 2 lb/1 kg)

2 ribs celery

1 Granny Smith apple

1 small yellow or red onion

2 small carrots, peeled

2 tablespoons cider vinegar

1¼ cups (10 fl oz/310 ml)
mayonnaise, preferably
homemade (page 216)

2 tablespoons minced fresh
flat-leaf parsley

Kosher salt and freshly
ground pepper

Sugar (optional)

SERVES 6–8

1 Cut the cabbage into wedges through the stem end, and cut out the core from each wedge. Using a food processor fitted with the slicing blade, slice the cabbage into thin slivers. Transfer to a large bowl. Then slice the celery the same way and add to the cabbage. (If you don't have a food processor with a slicing blade, thinly slice the cabbage and celery with a chef's knife.)

2 Replace the slicing blade with the shredding blade. Halve and core the apple but do not peel. Cut the apple and the onion into wedges. Shred the apple, onion, and carrots. Add to the cabbage and celery. (If you don't have a food processor with a shredding blade, shred the apple, onion, and carrots on the large holes of a box grater-shredder.)

3 Sprinkle the vegetables with the vinegar and toss to coat evenly. Add the mayonnaise and parsley. Mix well. Season with salt and pepper. If you prefer a sweeter coleslaw, stir in a little sugar until the flavor suits you.

4 Cover and refrigerate until chilled, at least 2 hours. Taste and adjust the seasoning with more vinegar, salt, and pepper before serving. Serve chilled.

Lexington-Style Red Slaw

1 head green cabbage
(about 2 lb/1 kg)

½ cup (4 fl oz/125 ml)
cider vinegar

½ cup (4 oz/125 g) ketchup

¼ cup (2 oz/60 g) sugar

Kosher salt and freshly
ground black pepper

1 teaspoon hot-pepper
sauce (optional)

SERVES 6–8

1 Cut the cabbage into wedges through the stem end, and cut out the core from each wedge. Using a food processor fitted with the slicing blade, slice the cabbage into thin slivers. You should have about 6 cups (18 oz/560 g). Transfer to a large bowl. (If you don't have a food processor with a slicing blade, thinly slice the cabbage with a chef's knife.)

2 In a large bowl, stir together the vinegar, ketchup, sugar, and ½ teaspoon salt until the sugar dissolves. Add the cabbage and toss with the dressing until evenly coated. Add 1 teaspoon black pepper and toss again. Taste for spiciness and add more black pepper or hot-pepper sauce, if desired.

3 Serve at once, or cover and refrigerate for up to 1 day before serving.

Asian-Style Slaw

6 tablespoons (3 oz/90 g) sugar

¼ cup (2 fl oz/60 ml) rice vinegar

2 tablespoons fresh lime juice

2 tablespoons chopped cilantro

1 tablespoon grated fresh ginger

1 jalapeño chile, seeded and finely chopped

4 cups (12 oz/375 g) shredded napa cabbage

1 carrot, peeled and shredded

SERVES 4–6

1 In a large bowl, whisk together the sugar, vinegar, and lime juice until the sugar dissolves. Add the cilantro, ginger, and chile. Whisk to combine.

2 Add the cabbage and carrot to the bowl and toss to coat evenly with the dressing. Let stand at room temperature for about 30 minutes before serving.

Cucumber Salad

3 tablespoons rice vinegar

1 tablespoon sugar

1 tablespoon canola oil

1 large English cucumber

½ small red onion

SERVES 4

1 In a large bowl, whisk together the vinegar and sugar until the sugar dissolves. Whisk in the oil.

2 Thinly slice the cucumber and onion. Add to the bowl and gently toss together. Cover and refrigerate for at least 15 minutes before serving.

Watermelon Salad

1 small seedless watermelon

5 oz (155 g) feta cheese, cubed

½ cup (½ oz/15 g) fresh basil leaves, chopped

¼ cup (2 fl oz/60 ml) extra-virgin olive oil

Juice of 1 lemon

Coarse sea salt and freshly ground pepper

SERVES 4–6

1 Cut the watermelon into thick slices, then cut off the rind, and cut the flesh into cubes. You should have about 3 cups (15 oz/470 g) cubes.

2 Spread the watermelon cubes on a platter. Sprinkle with the feta and basil. Drizzle with the oil and lemon juice, season with salt and pepper, and serve.

Chopped Salad

1 avocado, pitted and peeled

1 lemon wedge

½ cup (4 fl oz/125 ml) mayonnaise, preferably homemade (page 216)

1 small shallot, finely chopped

1 tablespoon *each* chopped fresh chives and chopped fresh flat-leaf parsley

Kosher salt and freshly ground pepper

4 slices thick-cut applewood-smoked bacon, chopped

4 cups (8 oz/250 g) chopped romaine lettuce hearts

2 cups (4 oz/125 g) chopped radicchio

1 red bell pepper, seeded and coarsely chopped

½ cup (2 oz/60 g) coarsely chopped red onion

SERVES 6–8

1 To make the dressing, in a bowl, mash the avocado with a fork, while squeezing in juice from the lemon wedge. Place the avocado in a blender, add the mayonnaise, and blend until smooth. Transfer to a bowl and stir in the shallot, chives, and parsley. Season with salt and pepper. Cover with plastic wrap and refrigerate until ready to use (no more than 4 hours).

2 In a frying pan over medium heat, fry the bacon until crisp, about 7 minutes. Transfer the bacon to paper towels to drain and cool.

3 In a large bowl, combine the bacon, romaine lettuce, radicchio, bell pepper, and onion and toss to mix. Add about ¼ cup (2 fl oz/60 ml) of the dressing and toss to mix well.

4 Divide the salad among plates, and pass the remaining dressing alongside for diners to use as desired.

Iceberg Wedge with Blue Cheese

4 slices thick-cut applewood-smoked bacon, chopped

1 head iceberg lettuce

16 cherry tomatoes, halved

4–6 oz (125–185 g) blue cheese, crumbled

½–¾ cup (4–6 fl oz/125–180 ml) Blue Cheese Dip (page 217), thinned to a dressing

¼ cup (½ oz/10 g) chopped fresh chives

Freshly ground pepper

SERVES 4

1 In a frying pan over medium heat, fry the bacon, stirring occasionally, until crisp and browned, about 7 minutes. Transfer to paper towels to drain and cool.

2 Cut the iceberg head into quarters through the stem end. Cut away the core from each quarter, and place each quarter on a salad plate.

3 Sprinkle the bacon evenly over each serving, then divide the cherry tomatoes and the blue cheese evenly among the plates.

4 Spoon about 2 tablespoons or more of the dressing over each serving and then sprinkle the salads evenly with the chives. Finally, grind pepper over each salad. These salads will hold for up to 30 minutes before serving.

Spinach and Bacon Salad

4 large eggs

10 oz (315 g) baby spinach, tough stems removed

8 slices thick-cut applewood-smoked bacon, chopped

3 tablespoons balsamic vinegar

1 tablespoon whole-grain mustard

2 tablespoons extra-virgin olive oil

Kosher salt and freshly ground pepper

1 small red onion, thinly sliced

1½ cups (9 oz/280 g) cherry tomatoes, halved

SERVES 6–8

1 To hard-boil the eggs, place them in a saucepan just large enough to hold them. Add cold water to cover by 1 inch (2.5 cm) and bring just to a boil over high heat. Remove the pan from the heat and cover. Let stand for 14 minutes. Drain the eggs, then transfer to a bowl of ice water, and let cool. Peel and coarsely chop the eggs.

2 Put the spinach in a large bowl. In a large frying pan over medium heat, fry the bacon, stirring occasionally, until crisp and browned, about 7 minutes. Using a slotted spoon, transfer to paper towels to drain. Pour off all but about 2 tablespoons of the fat from the pan. Off the heat, whisk the vinegar and mustard into the fat in the pan, then whisk in the oil. Season with salt and pepper. Drizzle over the spinach and toss to coat well.

3 Divide the spinach among individual plates, and top with the onion, tomatoes, and chopped eggs. Sprinkle with the bacon and serve at once.

Greek Salad

⅓ cup (3 fl oz/80 ml) red wine vinegar

1 clove garlic, pressed

Kosher salt and freshly ground black pepper

½ cup (4 fl oz/125 ml) extra-virgin olive oil

3 large, dead-ripe tomatoes

1 English cucumber

2 green onions, thinly sliced

5 oz (155 g) feta cheese, crumbled

20 Kalamata olives, pitted and quartered

½ cup (¾ oz/20 g) chopped fresh mint

SERVES 6–8

1 To make the vinaigrette, in a small bowl, whisk together the vinegar, garlic, ½ teaspoon salt, and ⅛ teaspoon pepper. Whisk in the olive oil until emulsified.

2 Core and seed the tomatoes and cut into wedges. Place in a large serving bowl. Peel the cucumber, cut in half lengthwise, and use a small spoon to scrape out the seeds. Cut the cucumber crosswise into slices, and add to the tomatoes. Add the green onions. Drizzle with half the vinaigrette and toss to coat evenly.

3 Sprinkle the salad with the feta, olives, and mint. Serve at once, passing the remaining dressing on the side.

Skillet Corn Bread

6 tablespoons (3 oz/90 g) unsalted butter, melted and cooled, plus more for greasing

1 cup (5 oz/155 g) all-purpose flour

1 cup (5 oz/155 g) yellow cornmeal, preferably stone-ground

2 tablespoons sugar

¾ teaspoon baking soda

½ teaspoon salt

⅔ cup (5 oz/155 g) sour cream or plain yogurt

⅔ cup (5 fl oz/160 ml) whole milk

2 large eggs

¾ cup (4½ oz/140 g) fresh or thawed frozen corn kernels

SERVES 6–8

1 Preheat the oven to 400°F (200°C). Grease a heavy 10-inch (25-cm) ovenproof frying pan (preferably cast iron) or a heavy 10-inch cake pan.

2 In a large bowl, whisk together the flour, cornmeal, sugar, baking soda, and salt. In another bowl, whisk together the sour cream, milk, and eggs until blended. Make a well in the center of the flour mixture, pour in the sour cream mixture and melted butter, and stir just until combined. Do not overmix. Fold in the corn kernels.

3 Pour the batter into the prepared pan and smooth the top. Bake until the corn bread is golden brown and a knife inserted into the center comes out clean, about 20 minutes.

4 Let cool in the pan for 5 minutes. Cut into wedges and serve hot or warm.

VARIATION To make chile-cheese cornbread, fold in ¾ cup (3 oz/90 g) shredded Cheddar cheese and 1 jalapeño chile, seeded and minced, or 1 can (4 oz/120 g) roasted mild green chiles, drained, along with the corn kernels.

Buttermilk Biscuits

1 cup (5 oz/155 g) all-purpose flour, plus more for dusting

1 cup (4 oz/125 g) cake flour

2 teaspoons baking powder

½ teaspoon baking soda

½ teaspoon salt

6 tablespoons (3 oz/90 g) cold unsalted butter, cut into 6 pieces

¾ cup (6 fl oz/180 ml) buttermilk

MAKES 6–8 BISCUITS

1 Preheat the oven to 400°F (200°C). Have ready a rimmed baking sheet.

2 In a bowl, sift together both flours, the baking powder, baking soda, and salt. Scatter the butter over the flour mixture. Using a pastry blender or 2 knives, cut in the butter until the mixture is the consistency of coarse crumbs the size of peas. Add the buttermilk and stir with a fork just until the dough comes together. Knead the dough a few times in the bowl.

3 Turn the dough out onto a lightly floured work surface. Using a light touch, pat out the dough into a round ¾ inch (2 cm) thick. Using a 2½-inch (6-cm) round biscuit cutter or cookie cutter, cut out as many rounds as possible. Place the rounds about 1 inch (2.5 cm) apart on the baking sheet. Gather up the dough scraps, pat them out again, cut out more dough rounds, and add them to the baking sheet.

4 Bake the biscuits until they have risen and are golden brown, 18–20 minutes. Serve hot or warm with plenty of butter.

Garlic Bread

3 cloves garlic, minced

3 tablespoons grated
Parmesan cheese

1 tablespoon minced fresh basil

Kosher salt

6 tablespoons (3 oz/90 g)
unsalted butter, at room
temperature

1 loaf country-style bread, split

1½ tablespoons minced fresh
flat-leaf parsley

SERVES 6–8

1 Preheat the oven to 450°F (230°C). In a small bowl, using a fork, work the garlic, Parmesan, basil, and ¼ teaspoon salt into the butter, distributing them evenly. Spread the mixture evenly onto the cut sides of the bread. Place the bread halves, cut side up, on a rimmed baking sheet.

2 Bake until the edges of the bread are toasted and the butter is melted, about 10 minutes.

3 Transfer to a cutting board and sprinkle evenly with the parsley. Cut crosswise into slices and serve hot.

VARIATION If you already have your grill set up for indirect grilling over medium or medium-high heat (page 16 or 19), you can grill-roast the garlic bread. Place the prepared bread halves, cut side up, on a rimmed baking sheet or piece of aluminum foil right on the grill. Cover and cook until the bread is lightly toasted and the butter is melted, about 10 minutes.

Buttery Dinner Rolls

1 package (2½ teaspoons)
active dry yeast

¼ cup (2 fl oz/60 ml) warm
water (105°–115°F/40°–46°C)

1 cup (8 fl oz/250 ml) whole milk

2 large eggs, at room
temperature, plus 1 egg,
beaten, for glaze

6 tablespoons (3 oz/90 g)
unsalted butter, at room
temperature, plus more
for greasing

4½ cups (22½ oz/705 g)
all-purpose flour, plus more
for kneading

2 tablespoons sugar

2 teaspoons salt

SERVES 8

1 In the bowl of a stand mixer, dissolve the yeast in the warm water and let stand until foamy, about 5 minutes. Add the milk, 2 eggs, butter, flour, sugar, and salt. Knead the dough on low speed using the dough hook attachment until smooth and elastic, 5–7 minutes.

2 Remove the dough from the bowl. Form the dough into a ball, transfer it to a lightly oiled bowl, and cover the bowl with plastic wrap. Let the dough rise in a warm, draft-free spot until it doubles in bulk, 1½–2 hours.

3 Heavily butter a rimmed baking sheet or line with parchment paper. Cut the dough in half, then cut each half into 8 equal pieces. Roll each piece against the work surface into a ball. Put the balls on the baking sheet, spacing them about ½ inch (12 mm) apart. Cover the baking sheet loosely with a kitchen towel, and let rise until puffy, 30–40 minutes.

4 Position a rack in the lower third of the oven, and preheat to 400°F (200°C). Brush the rolls lightly with the beaten egg. Bake until puffed and golden brown, about 20 minutes.

Sauces, Marinades, and Rubs

To be the master of the grill, you've got to make food with loads of flavor, and these sauces, marinades, and rubs will take your pork, beef, chicken, or seafood over the top. Feel free to mix and match the following recipes to create your own masterful dish.

All-Purpose BBQ Rub

¼ cup (2 oz/60 g) granulated sugar

1 tablespoon firmly packed light brown sugar

¼ cup (1 oz/30 g) paprika

1 tablespoon chile powder

1 teaspoon cayenne pepper

1 teaspoon smoked paprika

Kosher salt and freshly ground black pepper

MAKES ABOUT ⅔ CUP (5 OZ/155 G)

In a small container with a tight-fitting lid, stir together the sugars, paprika, chile powder, cayenne, smoked paprika, 1 teaspoon salt, and several grinds of black pepper. Cover and shake vigorously to mix. Use right away, or store in a cool, dark place for up to 1 month.

GOES GREAT WITH Pork tenderloin; pork or beef ribs; flank, skirt, or hanger steak; chicken

Latin Spice Rub

¼ cup (1 oz/30 g) ground cumin

2 tablespoons sugar

1 tablespoon ground coriander

Kosher salt and freshly ground pepper

MAKES ABOUT ½ CUP (4 OZ/125 G)

In a small container with a tight-fitting lid, stir together the cumin, sugar, coriander, 1½ teaspoons salt, and 3 tablespoons pepper. Cover and shake vigorously to mix. Use right away, or store in a cool, dark place for up to 1 month.

GOES GREAT WITH Skirt, hanger, or flank steak; pork tenderloin; fish

Cumin Crust Rub

¼ cup (1 oz/30 g) ground cumin

1 teaspoon smoked paprika

1 teaspoon firmly packed light brown sugar

¼ teaspoon ground coriander

¼ teaspoon cayenne pepper

Freshly ground black pepper

MAKES ABOUT ⅓ CUP (3 OZ/85 G)

In a small, dry frying pan over low heat, toast the cumin, stirring often, until aromatic, about 30 seconds. Pour onto a plate and let cool.

In a small container with a tight-fitting lid, stir together the cumin, paprika, sugar, coriander, cayenne pepper, and ½ teaspoon black pepper. Cover and shake vigorously to mix. Use right away, or store in a cool, dark place for up to 1 month.

GOES GREAT WITH Pork chops; chicken thighs; shrimp

Creole Spice Rub

½ cup (2 oz/60 g) paprika

6 tablespoons (1½ oz/45 g) granulated garlic

3 tablespoons granulated onion

3 tablespoons cayenne pepper

2 tablespoons dried oregano

2 tablespoons dried thyme

1 tablespoon smoked paprika

Kosher salt and freshly ground black pepper

MAKES ABOUT 1¾ CUPS (9 OZ/280 G)

In a small container with a tight-fitting lid, combine the paprika, granulated garlic and onion, cayenne pepper, oregano, thyme, smoked paprika, 6 tablespoons (2 oz/60 g)

salt, and 5 tablespoons (1½ oz/45 g) black pepper. Cover and shake vigorously to mix. Use right away, or store in a cool, dark place for up to 1 month.

GOES GREAT WITH Turkey breast; fish; shrimp

Cajun Seasoning

3 tablespoons granulated garlic

3 tablespoons granulated onion

3 tablespoons sweet paprika

1 tablespoon smoked paprika

1 tablespoon ground cayenne pepper

4 teaspoons dried oregano

4 teaspoons dried thyme

Kosher salt and freshly ground black pepper

MAKES ABOUT 1½ CUPS (8 OZ/250 G)

In a small container with a tight-fitting lid, stir together the garlic, onion, both paprikas, the cayenne pepper, oregano, thyme, and 3 tablespoons each salt and black pepper. Cover and shake vigorously to mix. Use right away, or store in a cool, dark place for up to 1 month.

GOES GREAT WITH Chicken breasts; fish; shrimp

North African Spice Rub

2 tablespoons smoked paprika

2 tablespoons firmly packed light brown sugar

1 tablespoon sesame seeds

1 tablespoon ground cinnamon

2 teaspoons *each* ground cumin and ground coriander

1 teaspoon *each* ground ginger and ground turmeric

½ teaspoon ground fenugreek

Kosher salt and freshly ground pepper

MAKES ABOUT ½ CUP (4 OZ/125 G)

In a small container with a tight-fitting lid, stir together the smoked paprika, brown sugar, sesame seeds, cinnamon, cumin, coriander, ginger, turmeric, fenugreek, 2 teaspoons salt, and 1 teaspoon pepper. Cover and shake vigorously to mix. Use right away, or store in a cool, dark place for up to 1 month.

GOES GREAT WITH Leg of lamb; chicken thighs

Caribbean Jerk Seasoning

3 green onions, including tender green parts, chopped

4 large cloves garlic, chopped

3 habanero chiles, seeded and chopped

¼ cup (2 fl oz/60 ml) fresh lime juice

3 tablespoons extra-virgin olive oil

2 tablespoons tamari or reduced-sodium soy sauce

1 tablespoon firmly packed light brown sugar

1 tablespoon chopped fresh thyme

2 teaspoons ground allspice

1 teaspoon ground nutmeg

½ teaspoon ground cinnamon

Kosher salt and freshly ground pepper

MAKES ABOUT 1 CUP (8 FL OZ/250 ML)

In a blender or food processor, combine the green onions, garlic, chiles, lime juice, oil, tamari, sugar, thyme, allspice, nutmeg, cinnamon, and 2 teaspoons each salt and pepper and then process until smooth. Use right away, or cover and refrigerate for up to 1 week.

GOES GREAT WITH Chicken skewers; pork tenderloin

Chipotle Spice Paste

¼ cup (2 fl oz/60 ml) olive oil

1 cup (1 oz/30 g) loosely packed fresh cilantro sprigs

4 cloves garlic, coarsely chopped

3 chipotle chiles in adobo sauce, chopped

2 tablespoons ground cumin

2 tablespoons ground coriander

1 tablespoon dry mustard

Kosher salt and freshly ground pepper

Fresh lime juice

MAKES ABOUT 1 CUP (8 FL OZ/250 ML)

In a blender or food processor, combine the olive oil, cilantro, garlic, chipotle chiles, cumin, coriander, mustard, 1 tablespoon salt, and 2 tablespoons pepper. Pulse to chop roughly, then process until smooth. Season to taste with lime juice. Use right away, or cover and refrigerate for up to 1 week.

GOES GREAT WITH Bone-in steaks; pork chops; bone-in chicken breasts or thighs

Herb Mop

½ cup (4 fl oz/125 ml) canola oil

¼ cup (2 fl oz/60 ml) tamari or reduced-sodium soy sauce

3 tablespoons red wine vinegar

2 tablespoons fresh lemon juice

2½ teaspoons Worcestershire sauce

2 cloves garlic, finely chopped

1½ tablespoons dry mustard

½ tablespoon dried parsley flakes

½ tablespoon dried rosemary

½ teaspoon dried oregano

¼ teaspoon dried thyme

Kosher salt and freshly ground pepper

MAKES ABOUT 2 CUPS (16 FL OZ/500 ML)

In a bowl, whisk together the canola oil, tamari, vinegar, lemon juice, Worcestershire sauce, garlic, mustard, parsley, rosemary, oregano, thyme, 1 teaspoon salt, and 1 teaspoon pepper, mixing well. Use right away, or store in an airtight container in the refrigerator for up to 6 weeks. Shake or whisk well before using. It can also be used as a marinade.

GOES GREAT WITH Chicken (whole or breast); turkey

Balsamic-Mustard Marinade

¼ cup (2 fl oz/60 ml) tamari or reduced-sodium soy sauce

¼ cup (2 fl oz/60 ml) extra-virgin olive oil

¼ cup (2 fl oz/60 ml) balsamic vinegar

6 cloves garlic, finely minced or pressed

2 tablespoons whole-grain mustard

1 tablespoon Dijon mustard

1 tablespoon yellow or brown mustard seeds

2 teaspoons peeled and grated fresh ginger

Kosher salt and freshly ground pepper

MAKES ABOUT ¾ CUP (6 FL OZ/180 ML)

In a small bowl, combine the tamari, oil, vinegar, garlic, mustards, mustard seeds, ginger, 1 teaspoon pepper, and a pinch of salt. Use right away, or cover and refrigerate for up to 1 day before using.

GOES GREAT WITH Skirt, hanger, or flank steak; chicken

Rosemary-Lemon Marinade

¾ cup (6 fl oz/180 ml) olive oil

⅓ cup (3 fl oz/80 ml) red wine vinegar

¼ cup (2 fl oz/60 ml) fresh lemon juice

1 tablespoon finely chopped fresh rosemary

2 teaspoons sugar

1 clove garlic, pressed

½ teaspoon freshly ground pepper

MAKES ABOUT 1½ CUPS (12 FL OZ/375 ML)

In a bowl, stir together the oil, vinegar, lemon juice, rosemary, sugar, garlic, and pepper. Use right away, or cover and refrigerate for up to 1 day before using.

GOES GREAT WITH Top sirloin; lamb; chicken breasts; fish; vegetables

Ginger-Soy Marinade

¼ cup (2 fl oz/60 ml) Worcestershire sauce

3 tablespoons soy sauce

2 tablespoons fresh lemon juice

1 tablespoon hoisin sauce

2 tablespoons chopped fresh cilantro

1 tablespoon peeled and minced fresh ginger

Freshly ground pepper

MAKES ABOUT ¾ CUP (6 FL OZ/180 ML)

In a small bowl, stir together the Worcestershire sauce, soy sauce, lemon juice, hoisin sauce, cilantro, ginger, and a few grinds of pepper. Use right away, or cover and refrigerate for up to 1 day before using.

GOES GREAT WITH Skirt, hanger, or flank steak; duck

Greek Marinade

½ cup (4 fl oz/125 ml) fresh lemon juice

4 cloves garlic, pressed

2 tablespoons chopped fresh flat-leaf parsley

1 tablespoon *each* chopped fresh oregano, fresh rosemary, fresh thyme, and fresh basil

½ cup (4 fl oz/125 ml) olive oil

MAKES ABOUT 1¼ CUPS (10 FL OZ/300 ML)

In a bowl, stir together the lemon juice, garlic, parsley, oregano, rosemary, thyme, and basil, then whisk in the oil. Use right away, or cover and refrigerate for up to 1 day before using.

GOES GREAT WITH Chicken; vegetables

Bourbon-Orange Marinade

⅓ cup (3 fl oz/80 ml) bourbon or Tennessee sipping whiskey

⅓ cup (3½ oz/105 g) orange marmalade, gently heated

2 tablespoons firmly packed dark brown sugar

2 tablespoons fresh orange juice

2 cloves garlic, finely minced

4 whole cloves

Freshly ground pepper

MAKES ABOUT ¾ CUP (6 FL OZ/180 ML)

In a small bowl, stir together the bourbon, marmalade, sugar, orange juice, garlic, cloves, and a few grinds of pepper. Use right away, or cover and refrigerate for up to 1 day before using.

GOES GREAT WITH Pork spareribs; pork chops; duck

Asian-Style Glaze

⅔ cup (5 oz/155 g) ketchup

⅔ cup (5 fl oz/160 ml) orange juice

3 tablespoons black bean–garlic sauce

2 tablespoons chile-garlic sauce

2 tablespoons peeled and minced fresh ginger

2 tablespoons dry sherry

1 tablespoon firmly packed light brown sugar

1 tablespoon granulated sugar

1 tablespoon Asian sesame oil

1 tablespoon tamari or reduced-sodium soy sauce

MAKES ABOUT 2 CUPS (16 FL OZ/500 ML)

In a bowl, stir together the ketchup, orange juice, both garlic sauces, ginger, sherry, both sugars, sesame oil, and tamari, mixing well. Use right away, or cover and refrigerate for up to 2 days.

GOES GREAT WITH Baby back ribs; chicken wings

Basic Poultry Brine

5 tablespoons (2½ oz/75 g) kosher salt

2 tablespoons dried basil

2 tablespoons coriander seeds

1 tablespoon peppercorns

1 tablespoon yellow mustard seeds

1 teaspoon granulated garlic

2 bay leaves

MAKES ABOUT 8 CUPS (64 FL OZ/2 L), OR ENOUGH FOR 1 CHICKEN

In a large bowl, combine 8 cups (64 fl oz/2 l) water, the salt, basil, coriander, peppercorns, mustard seeds, granulated garlic, and bay leaves and stir until the salt dissolves. Use right away.

Basic Pork Brine

¼ cup (2 fl oz/60 ml) cider vinegar

¼ cup (2 oz/60 g) firmly packed brown sugar

1 teaspoon dried thyme

1 teaspoon juniper berries (optional)

⅛ teaspoon red pepper flakes

Kosher salt and freshly ground black pepper

MAKES ABOUT 6½ CUPS (1.75 L), OR ENOUGH FOR 4–6 PORK CHOPS

In a large bowl, combine 6 cups (48 fl oz/1.5 l) water, the vinegar, sugar, thyme, juniper berries, red pepper flakes, 2 tablespoons salt, and 1 tablespoon black pepper and stir until the sugar and salt dissolve. Use right away.

Basic Shrimp Brine

½ cup (4 oz/125 g) kosher salt

2 tablespoons sugar

1 teaspoon ground cumin

1 teaspoon ground coriander

MAKES ABOUT 6 CUPS (48 FL OZ/1.5 L), OR ENOUGH FOR 2 LB (1 KG) SHRIMP

In a large bowl, combine 6 cups (48 fl oz/1.5 l) water, the salt, sugar, cumin, and coriander and stir to dissolve the salt and sugar. Use right away.

Lexington-Style Dip

1 qt (1 l) cider vinegar

1½ cups (12 oz/375 g) ketchup

1 cup (8 oz/250 g) plus 1 tablespoon granulated sugar

1 tablespoon firmly packed light brown sugar

1 tablespoon red pepper flakes

½ teaspoon cayenne pepper

Kosher salt and freshly ground black pepper

MAKES ABOUT 1 QT (1 L)

Pour the vinegar into a saucepan. Stir in the ketchup, both sugars, red pepper flakes, cayenne, 2 tablespoons salt, and ½ teaspoon black pepper. Rinse the measuring pitcher used for the ketchup with ¾ cup (6 fl oz/180 ml) water and add to the pan. Place over medium heat, bring to a gentle simmer, and cook slowly, stirring often, for 30 minutes. Never let the mixture boil.

Raise the heat to medium-high. A red foam will begin to build on top. When the foam completely covers the surface, the "dip" is done. Remove from the heat and let cool. Use right away, or store in an airtight container in the refrigerator for up to 6 weeks.

GOES GREAT WITH Pulled pork

Classic BBQ Sauce

1 cup (8 oz/250 g) ketchup

2 tablespoons yellow mustard

1 tablespoon cider vinegar

2 teaspoons firmly packed dark brown sugar

½ cup (4 fl oz/125 ml) low-sodium chicken broth

Kosher salt and freshly ground pepper

2 chipotle chiles in adobo sauce, finely chopped (optional)

¼ teaspoon ground cumin (optional)

MAKES ABOUT 2 CUPS (16 FL OZ/500 ML)

In a saucepan over medium heat, combine the ketchup, mustard, vinegar, sugar, broth, a pinch of salt, and 2 teaspoons pepper and bring to a simmer, stirring to dissolve the sugar. For a Southwest-style sauce, stir in the chiles and cumin. Simmer for 5 minutes for a relatively thin sauce or for 10–15 minutes for a thick sauce. Taste and adjust the seasoning with salt.

Use right away, or let cool and store in an airtight container in the refrigerator for up to 1 month.

GOES GREAT WITH Burgers; ribs; chicken; oysters

Perfect Brisket BBQ Sauce

2 tablespoons margarine (not butter)

¼ cup (1½ oz/45 g) finely chopped yellow onion

1 clove garlic, pressed

1 cup (8 oz/250 g) ketchup

¼ cup (2 oz/60 g) firmly packed light brown sugar

¼ cup (2 fl oz/60 ml) fresh lemon juice

1 tablespoon Worcestershire sauce

1 tablespoon yellow mustard

MAKES ABOUT 2 CUPS (16 FL OZ/500 ML)

In a small saucepan over medium heat, melt the margarine. Add the onion and garlic and cook, stirring, until softened but not colored, about 3 minutes. Stir in the ketchup, sugar, lemon juice, Worcestershire, and mustard and bring to a boil. Reduce the heat to low and simmer, uncovered, until thickened, 15–20 minutes.

Use right away, or let cool and store in an airtight container in the refrigerator for up to 2 weeks.

GOES GREAT WITH Brisket; beef ribs

Asian-Style BBQ Sauce

¼ cup (2 fl oz/60 ml) hoisin sauce

¼ cup (2 fl oz/60 ml) sweet-hot pepper sauce

2 tablespoons mirin

1 tablespoon Asian sesame oil

MAKES ABOUT 1 CUP (8 FL OZ/250 ML)

In a bowl, whisk together the hoisin, pepper sauce, mirin, sesame oil, and ¼ cup (2 fl oz/60 ml) water. Taste and adjust with more sesame oil, if desired.

Use right away, or store in an airtight container in the refrigerator for up to 2 months. Bring to room temperature before using.

GOES GREAT WITH Beef short ribs; baby back ribs

Coffee BBQ Sauce

¼ cup (2 fl oz/60 ml) canola oil

1 yellow onion, chopped

10 cloves garlic, coarsely chopped

¾ cup (3 oz/90 g) dark-roast whole coffee beans

¼ cup (⅓ oz/10 g) chopped fresh cilantro

1 jalapeño chile, seeded and chopped

1 teaspoon *each* ground cumin and red pepper flakes

¼ cup (2 oz/60 g) firmly packed dark brown sugar

¾ cup (6 fl oz/180 ml) red wine vinegar

1 cup (8 oz/250 g) ketchup

3 cans (6 oz/185 g *each*) tomato paste

Kosher salt and freshly ground black pepper

MAKES ABOUT 2 CUPS (16 FL OZ/500 ML)

In a saucepan over medium heat, warm the oil. Add the onion, garlic, coffee, cilantro, chile, cumin, and red pepper flakes and cook, stirring, for 2 minutes. Add the sugar, vinegar, and ketchup, and cook, stirring occasionally, until the liquid has reduced by one-fourth, 15 minutes. Add the tomato paste and 1 tablespoon each salt and pepper and stir well. Cover, reduce the heat to low, and simmer gently for 1 hour to blend the flavors. Remove from the heat and strain through a sieve into a bowl. Let cool. Use right away, or store in an airtight container in the refrigerator for up to 1 month.

GOES GREAT WITH Beef ribs; pork loin; pork chops

Bourbon Steak Sauce

½ cup (4 oz/125 g) Dijon mustard

¼ cup (2 oz/60 g) ketchup

3 tablespoons steak sauce, preferably A1

2 tablespoons bourbon

2 tablespoons well-drained prepared horseradish

1 tablespoon *each* Worcestershire sauce, pure maple syrup, dark corn syrup, and tamari or reduced-sodium soy sauce

4 anchovy fillets, mashed to a paste

Kosher salt and freshly ground pepper

MAKES ABOUT 1½ CUPS (12 FL OZ/375 ML)

In a bowl, mix together the mustard, ketchup, steak sauce, bourbon, horseradish, Worcestershire, maple syrup, corn syrup, tamari, and anchovies. Season with salt and pepper. Use right away, or store in an airtight container in the refrigerator for up to 1 week. Bring to room temperature or warm slightly before serving.

GOES GREAT WITH Bone-in steaks; burgers

Teriyaki Sauce

½ cup (4 fl oz/125 ml) pineapple juice

¼ cup (2 fl oz/60 ml) *each* tamari or reduced-sodium soy sauce and Worcestershire sauce

2 tablespoons dry sherry

⅛ teaspoon ground ginger

¼ teaspoon garlic salt

MAKES ABOUT 1 CUP (8 FL OZ/250 ML)

In a saucepan, combine the pineapple juice, tamari, Worcestershire, ¼ cup (2 fl oz/60 ml) water, sherry, ginger, and garlic salt. Place over medium-high heat and bring to a boil. Reduce the heat to medium-low and simmer, stirring, until thickened, 10–12 minutes. Use right away or store in an airtight container in the refrigerator for up to 1 week.

GOES GREAT WITH Top sirloin; chicken; vegetables

Pesto

1 cup (1 oz/30 g) tightly packed fresh basil leaves

½ cup (½ oz/15 g) fresh flat-leaf parsley leaves

1 tablespoon pine nuts

Pinch of red pepper flakes

Finely grated zest of 1 lemon

1 tablespoon grated Asiago or Parmesan cheese

½ cup (4 fl oz/125 ml) extra-virgin olive oil

MAKES ABOUT 1 CUP (8 FL OZ/250 ML)

In a blender or food processor, combine the basil, parsley, and pine nuts and pulse briefly to combine. Add the red pepper flakes, lemon zest, and cheese and pulse just to mix. With the machine running, slowly add the oil and process until smooth. Use right away, or transfer to a jar or other airtight container, top with a thin layer of oil, cover tightly, and refrigerate for up to 1 week. Bring to room temperature before using.

GOES GREAT WITH Chicken breasts; fish; vegetables

Mint-Feta Pesto

1 cup (1 oz/30 g) loosely packed fresh mint leaves

2 tablespoons pine nuts

⅛ teaspoon red pepper flakes

½ cup (4 fl oz/125 ml) extra-virgin olive oil, plus more if needed

6 oz (185 g) feta cheese, crumbled

Kosher salt and freshly ground black pepper

MAKES ABOUT ¾ CUP (6 FL OZ/180 ML)

In a blender or food processor, combine the mint, pine nuts, and red pepper flakes and pulse until the mint is chopped. With the machine running, slowly add the oil in a thin, steady stream, processing until a thin paste forms. If the paste is too thick, add a little more oil. Add the feta cheese and pulse 3 or 4 times to mix. Alternatively, for a more rustic sauce, transfer the mint mixture to a bowl and stir in the feta just until combined. Season with salt and black pepper.

Use right away, or cover and refrigerate for up to 3 days. Bring to room temperature and stir just before serving.

GOES GREAT WITH Lamb burgers or chops; vegetables

Mediterranean Tapenade

1 cup (5 oz/155 g) pitted good-quality black or green olives

¼ cup (2 oz/60 g) diced olive oil–packed sun-dried tomatoes

¼ cup (2 fl oz/60 ml) extra-virgin olive oil

8 fresh basil leaves

1 tablespoon pine nuts

2 teaspoons grated lemon zest

⅛ teaspoon red pepper flakes

Kosher salt and freshly ground black pepper

MAKES 1½ CUPS (12 OZ/375 G)

In a food processor, combine the olives, tomatoes, oil, basil, pine nuts, lemon zest, and red pepper flakes and pulse until a paste forms. Transfer to a small bowl and season with salt and black pepper. The tapenade tastes best if made a day in advance. It will keep, covered and refrigerated, for up to 3 days.

GOES GREAT WITH Lamb; meaty fish; vegetables

Chimichurri

½ cup (4 fl oz/125 ml) *each* extra-virgin olive oil and red wine vinegar

¼ cup (1½ oz/45 g) finely chopped red onion

2 tablespoons *each* finely chopped red bell pepper and finely chopped fresh flat-leaf parsley

2 teaspoons *each* finely chopped fresh oregano and garlic

¼ teaspoon red pepper flakes

Kosher salt and freshly ground black pepper

MAKES ABOUT 1 CUP (8 FL OZ/250 ML)

In a bowl, whisk together the oil, vinegar, onion, bell pepper, parsley, oregano, garlic, red pepper flakes, a pinch of salt, and a few grinds of black pepper. Let stand at room temperature for about 30 minutes to allow the flavors to blend. Whisk again just before serving. Or, cover and refrigerate for up to 2 days. Bring to room temperature before serving.

GOES GREAT WITH Beef tenderloin; bone-in steaks

Smoky Tomato Salsa

3 large, ripe tomatoes, thickly sliced

1 small red onion, thickly sliced

1 jalapeño chile, halved lengthwise and seeded

Olive oil for drizzling

Juice of 2 limes

¼ cup (⅓ oz/10 g) finely chopped fresh cilantro

Kosher salt and freshly ground pepper

MAKES ABOUT 1½ CUPS (9 OZ/280 G)

Prepare a charcoal or gas grill for direct grilling over high heat (page 16 or 18). Brush and oil the grill grate.

Drizzle the tomato and onion slices and chile halves with oil. Place on the grill and cook, turning once, until some nice char develops, about 2 minutes per side. Remove from the grill, chop coarsely, and place in a bowl. Stir in the lime juice and cilantro. Divide the mixture in half, puree half of it in a food processor, then return to the bowl. Mix well and season with salt and pepper. The salsa tastes best if made a day in advance. It will keep, covered and refrigerated, for up to 1 week.

GOES GREAT WITH Tri-tip; steak or chicken tacos

Grilled Pineapple Salsa

½ fresh pineapple, peeled, cored, and cut into rings

1 red onion, thickly sliced

Olive oil for drizzling

1 jalapeño chile

½ avocado, peeled and diced

1 tablespoon finely chopped fresh mint

Juice of 1 lime

Kosher salt

MAKES ABOUT 1 CUP (6 OZ/185 G)

Prepare a charcoal or gas grill for direct grilling over high heat (page 16 or 18). Brush and oil the grill grate.

Drizzle the pineapple and onion slices with oil, then place on the grill with the jalapeño. Cook the pineapple and onion slices, turning once, until they are grill marked and are heated through, about 8 minutes total. Cook the chile, turning, until charred on all sides.

Transfer the pineapple, onion, and chile to a cutting board. Chop the pineapple and onion into chunks and place in a bowl. When the chile is cool enough to handle, peel, stem, seed, and dice it, then add it to the bowl. Add the avocado and mint and stir to mix. Add the lime juice, stir again, and then season with salt.

Use right away, or cover and refrigerate for up to 2 days. Bring to room temperature before serving.

GOES GREAT WITH Chicken legs; meaty fish

Pico de Gallo

3 large, ripe tomatoes, chopped

½ cup (2½ oz/75 g) diced red onion

½ cup (¾ oz/20 g) minced fresh cilantro

1 jalapeño chile, seeded and diced

Juice of 3 limes

Kosher salt

MAKES ABOUT 1½ CUPS (9 OZ/280 G)

In a bowl, stir together the tomatoes, onion, cilantro, chile, and lime juice. Season with salt. Let sit at room temperature for at least 1 hour to allow the flavors to blend. The salsa will keep in an airtight container in the refrigerator for up to 3 days.

GOES GREAT WITH Tri-tip; steak or chicken tacos

Creamy Avocado Salsa

½ cup (4 oz/125 g) sour cream

2 teaspoons whole-grain mustard

2 teaspoons white wine vinegar or Champagne vinegar

1 avocado, halved, pitted, peeled, and cut into small chunks

Kosher salt and freshly ground pepper

MAKES ABOUT 1 CUP (8 OZ/250 G)

In a bowl, whisk together the sour cream, mustard, and vinegar. Carefully fold in the avocado, then season with salt and pepper. Use right away, or cover and refrigerate for up to 2 days.

GOES GREAT WITH Steak, chicken, or fish tacos

Spicy Tomato Jam

1 tablespoon canola oil

1 clove garlic, finely chopped

2 large tomatoes, peeled, seeded, and coarsely chopped

1 fresh thyme sprig

½ cup (4 fl oz/125 ml) reduced-sodium chicken broth

½ teaspoon Worcestershire sauce

⅛ teaspoon red pepper flakes

Kosher salt and freshly ground black pepper

MAKES ABOUT ¾ CUP (7½ OZ/235 G)

In a saucepan over medium heat, warm the oil. Add the garlic and cook, stirring, for 1 minute. Add the tomatoes and cook, stirring, for 3 minutes. Stir in the thyme, broth, Worcestershire, and red pepper flakes, and simmer until the tomatoes have cooked down, about 15 minutes. Season with salt and black pepper. Remove from the heat, and remove and discard the thyme sprig. Let cool. Use right away, or cover and refrigerate for up to 4 days. Bring to room temperature before serving.

GOES GREAT WITH Bone-in pork chops; corn bread

Bacon-Onion Jam

3 slices thick-cut applewood-smoked bacon

½ cup (2 oz/60 g) chopped sweet onion

1 fresh thyme sprig

1 teaspoon whole-grain mustard

1½-oz (45-g) block veal demi-glace

¼ cup (2 fl oz/60 ml) reduced-sodium chicken broth

Kosher salt and freshly ground pepper

MAKES ABOUT 1 CUP (10 OZ/315 G)

In a frying pan over medium heat, fry the bacon until crisp, about 5 minutes. Transfer the bacon to paper towels to drain, then chop and set aside. Add the onion to the fat remaining in the pan and cook over medium heat, stirring, until caramelized, about 15 minutes. Add the thyme, mustard, demi-glace, and broth and cook until the mixture has begun to thicken, about 15 minutes. Stir in the bacon and season with salt and pepper. Use right away, or cover and refrigerate for up to 4 days. Bring to room temperature before serving.

GOES GREAT WITH Bone-in pork chops; pork tenderloin; corn bread

Homemade Mayonnaise

1 large egg, fresh or pasteurized

1 tablespoon fresh lemon juice

1 teaspoon Dijon mustard

Kosher salt

¾ cup (6 fl oz/180 ml) olive oil

¾ cup (6 fl oz/180 ml) canola oil

MAKES ABOUT 1½ CUPS (12 FL OZ/375 ML)

In a food processor or a blender, combine the egg, lemon juice, mustard, and ¼ teaspoon salt. Combine the oils in a glass measuring pitcher. With the machine running, slowly add the oil mixture in a thin, steady stream and process until the mayonnaise is thick. Add 1 tablespoon warm water and process briefly. Taste and adjust the seasoning.

Use right away, or refrigerate in an airtight container for up to 3 days.

GOES GREAT WITH Asparagus; potatoes

Simple Béarnaise Sauce

6 large egg yolks

1 cup (8 oz/250 g) unsalted butter

Juice of 1 lemon

⅛ teaspoon ground cayenne pepper

Kosher salt

1 tablespoon chopped fresh tarragon

½ teaspoon tarragon vinegar or white wine vinegar

MAKES ABOUT 1½ CUPS (12 FL OZ/375 ML)

In a blender, process the egg yolks until creamy and pale yellow. In a small saucepan over low heat, melt the butter. Watch it closely because you don't want the solids to separate from the liquid. Add the lemon juice and cayenne pepper, raise the heat to medium, and bring to a boil. Remove from the heat and pour into a small pitcher. With the blender running at medium speed, slowly pour the hot butter mixture into the egg yolks and process until smooth. Season with ½ teaspoon salt. In the pitcher, mix together the tarragon, vinegar, and 3 tablespoons hot water. Add enough of the hot water mixture to achieve a good consistency. Serve right away, or pour into a thermos and set aside at room temperature. The sauce will stay warm for up to 4 hours.

GOES GREAT WITH Filets mignons; fish; asparagus

Fresh Horseradish Sauce

¼ cup (2 fl oz/60 ml) mayonnaise, preferably homemade (see left)

½ cup (4 oz/125 g) sour cream

3 tablespoons freshly grated horseradish root

2 tablespoons chopped fresh chives

1 teaspoon each English mustard and steak sauce

MAKES ABOUT 1 CUP (8 OZ/250 G)

In a small bowl, stir together the mayonnaise, sour cream, horseradish, chives, mustard, and steak sauce.

Use right away, or cover and refrigerate for up to 3 days, then bring to room temperature before serving. (The sauce tastes best if made a day ahead.)

GOES GREAT WITH Prime rib; steaks; pork roast

Blue Cheese Dip

1 cup (8 oz/250 g) sour cream

¼ cup (2 fl oz/60 ml) mayonnaise, preferably homemade (page 216)

1 tablespoon Worcestershire sauce

1 tablespoon fresh lemon juice

1 teaspoon steak sauce

2 cloves garlic, finely minced, then crushed to a paste

2 tablespoons chopped fresh chives

⅛ teaspoon cayenne pepper

1 cup (5 oz/155 g) crumbled blue cheese

Kosher salt and freshly ground black pepper

About 2 tablespoons whole milk, if needed

MAKES ABOUT 3 CUPS (24 FL OZ/875 ML)

In a bowl, combine the sour cream, mayonnaise, Worcestershire, lemon juice, steak sauce, garlic, chives, and cayenne pepper and fold together until well mixed. Fold in the cheese, then season with salt and black pepper.

Cover and refrigerate until serving. The dip tastes best if made a day head and will keep for up to 2 weeks. To use as a salad dressing, thin with milk to the desired consistency.

GOES GREAT WITH Chicken wings; vegetables

Spicy Peanut Sauce

2 cups (16 fl oz/500 ml) coconut milk

¼ cup (1½ oz/45 g) chopped unsalted dry-roasted peanuts

2 tablespoons all-natural creamy peanut butter

2 tablespoons Asian fish sauce

1 tablespoon seedless tamarind paste, or 1 teaspoon fresh lime juice

2 tablespoons firmly packed light brown sugar

1½ teaspoons green curry paste

1 teaspoon paprika

1 clove garlic, finely minced, then crushed to a paste

MAKES ABOUT 2 CUPS (16 FL OZ/500 ML)

In a saucepan over medium heat, combine the coconut milk, peanuts, peanut butter, fish sauce, tamarind paste, sugar, curry paste, paprika, and garlic. Bring to a gentle simmer, stirring constantly to blend the ingredients thoroughly, then cook, stirring occasionally, until thickened and reduced by half, 15–20 minutes. Set aside off the heat. Serve warm or at room temperature.

GOES GREAT WITH Chicken skewers; flank steak

Coconut-Lime Sauce

1 jalapeño chile, seeded and coarsely chopped

1 tablespoon canola oil

1 small red onion, coarsely chopped

3 cloves garlic, coarsely chopped

1 can (14 fl oz/430 ml) coconut milk

¼ cup (2 fl oz/60 ml) cream of coconut

¼ cup (2 fl oz/60 ml) fresh lime juice

1 teaspoon honey

Kosher salt and freshly ground pepper

MAKES ABOUT 2 CUPS (16 FL OZ/500 ML)

Place a saucepan over medium-high heat. Throw in the chile and heat, stirring occasionally, until the chile takes on a little color, about 2 minutes. Add the oil, and then add the onion and garlic and cook, stirring often, until soft but not browned, about 5 minutes. Pour in the coconut milk and cream of coconut, bring to a simmer, adjust the heat to maintain the simmer, and cook for 10 minutes to blend the flavors. Remove from the heat. For a rustic sauce, leave as is. For a more refined sauce, transfer to a blender and process until smooth, then return to the pan. Mix in the lime juice and honey, and season with salt and pepper.

Use right away, or cover and refrigerate for up to 1 day. Reheat gently before serving.

GOES GREAT WITH Fish; shrimp

Index

weldonowen

415 Jackson Street, Suite 200, San Francisco, CA 94111
Telephone: 415 291 0100 Fax: 415 291 8841
wopublishing.com

GRILL MASTER

Conceived and produced by Weldon Owen, Inc.
In collaboration with Williams-Sonoma, Inc.

A WELDON OWEN PRODUCTION

Copyright © 2011 Weldon Owen, Inc. and Williams-Sonoma, Inc.
All rights reserved, including the right of reproduction
in whole or in part in any form.

Color separations by Embassy Graphics in Canada
Printed and bound by Toppan Leefung Printing Limited in China

First printed in 2011
10 9 8 7 6 5 4 3 2 1

Library of Congress Cataloging-in Publication
data is available.

ISBN 13: 978-1-61628-059-8
ISBN 10: 1-61628-059-X

Weldon Owen is a division of
BONNIER

WELDON OWEN, INC.

CEO and President Terry Newell
VP, Sales and Marketing Amy Kaneko
Director of Finance Mark Perrigo

VP and Publisher Hannah Rahill
Executive Editor Kim Laidlaw
Associate Editor Julia Nelson

Creative Director Emma Boys
Art Director Alexandra Zeigler
Associate Art Director Diana Heom

Production Director Chris Hemesath
Production Manager Michelle Duggan
Color Manager Teri Bell

Photographer Ray Kachatorian
Food Stylist Jamie Kimm
Prop Stylist Christine Wolheim

ACKNOWLEDGMENTS

From Fred Thompson: This book is dedicated to Kyle and Laura—I couldn't be prouder of you both. No book is truly the work of one person, and I had plenty of help to share the stress, chaos, joy, and love that went into writing *Grill Master*. Kyle Wilkerson was my hands-on brain trust for this book, keeping me honest and creative. I call him "The King of Meat" for his grilling abilities. We had a blast working on this book and I can't thank him enough. Belinda Ellis, editor for *Edible Piedmont Magazine*, friend, and food confidant, was undergoing treatment for cancer during this process, yet still gamely participated, even when the smell of smoke was not what she needed. Thankfully, she is now a cancer survivor. All the wonderful folks at Weldon Owen who have made writing a cookbook a breeze, especially Hannah Rahill, Kim Laidlaw, and Julia Nelson. Their professionalism makes my task easier. Ray Kachatorian's photographs will make you hungry and want to rush to the grill. His excellent eye has captured every facet of my words in a way few could. Thanks. Food stylist Jamie Kimm represents the recipes in an honest and beautiful way. Nikki Parrish again endured my lack of word processing skill, helping to get the manuscript together. My neighborhood gang of taste-testers put their mouths in danger, as they have for all my cookbooks, to help me know when a recipe is finally prefect. Inspiration came from a wealth of people and you will get to know them as you cook from this tome. And of course, I'd like to thank Williams-Sonoma. Most of all, thanks to you, the reader, for letting me invade your backyard.

Weldon Owen would like to thank the following individuals for their kind assistance in making this book: Kimberly Chun, Conor Collins, Scott Hove, Cathy Lee, Elizabeth Parson, Dennis Rogers, Sharon Silva, Christian Stark, and Jason Wheeler.